HOT ICE

THEATRE FOR CLASSICAL AND CHRISTIAN SCHOOLS

LEVEL I: ANCIENT

Student's Edition

EILEEN CUNNINGHAM

MARCEE COSBY

ISBN: 978-0692731055

Table of Contents

INTRODUCTION

Purpose

Though there are textbooks aplenty for the instruction of drama in middle schools and high schools, we could find little that was written with the curriculum and methodology of classical education in mind. Nor could we find much that reflected the Christian worldview. The purpose of this book, therefore, is to fill the need of students, teachers, and families involved in classical and Christian education. Specifically, the book introduces drama to students in grades 7-12. As a textbook for Christian families, it attempts to explain the sometimes hostile relationship between the stage and the Church and directs students' attention to the moral and ethical responsibilities of the theatre community. It explains why drama is important for students of classical antiquity, and provides focus for young people who wish to turn the talents God has given them back into His service in the form of theatre arts.

As a textbook for classical education, *Hot Ice* employs primary sources, integrates literature and history, examines the origins of drama in the Golden Age of Greece, identifies developments made by the Romans in both the Republic and the Empire, and examines passages from classical plays from the perspective of the progymnasmata and other rhetorical techniques. It addresses the classical trivium and—from the quadrivium—music as an aspect of theatre. There are spots in which familiarity with Latin and Greek might be helpful, but there is nothing that should prevent a student who does not know these languages from receiving benefit from the book.

We endeavor to stay true to the teaching of Scripture, which says, "And whatever you do, in word or deed, do everything in the name of the Lord Jesus, giving thanks to God the Father through him" (Col. 3:17).

The Title *Hot Ice*

At the end of *A Midsummer Night's Dream* by William Shakespeare, Bottom and the other "mechanicals" present a play to celebrate the wedding of Duke Theseus. Musing over the oxymorons in the handbill of the play, Theseus speaks.

THESEUS:
[Reading] "A tedious brief scene of young Pyramus
And his love Thisbe; very tragical mirth."
Merry and tragical! tedious and brief!
That is, hot ice and wondrous strange snow.
How shall we find the concord of this discord? (5.1.56-60)

The lines resound with meaning for the lover of literature and of drama, in particular, for they come not just from a play, but from a play within a play, which was written, not by any ordinary playwright, but by the greatest master of the English language ever to set pen to paper. The phrase *hot ice* is particularly apt, as it typifies the wonderful diction of the playwright, calls up the thrill of the stage, and suits, as well, the iconic theatre masks of comedy and tragedy. For these reasons, we selected the phrase *Hot Ice* as the title of this book, which we hope will both inform and inspire a new generation of thespians.

Bible References

Unless otherwise noted, all Scripture in this book is from the English Standard Version of the Bible.

Editing

Some translations of plays written originally in Greek and Latin were made in the nineteenth century, so, since they are in the public domain, we have taken the liberty of editing material for the spelling and conventions of Standard Written English as it is taught in schools in our times. We readily confess to tampering with British spellings (changing *–our* to *–or,* for example), but we have ardently committed ourselves to the French *–re* suffix on the word *theatre.* Call us snooty if you must, but we allow that, like broken clocks, the French and British can be right twice per day, and, besides, seeing the word spelled as *theater* has on us the same effect as squeaky chalk on a blackboard. Light editing of public domain material has also been done occasionally to suit the age of the reader.

Contact Us

If you have questions or comments, please feel free to contact us via our web site: <http://www.writingtheclassicalway.com>.

WHY DRAMA?

Chapter 1

Introduction

Dorothy L. Sayers, a friend of C. S. Lewis and the Inklings, began her essay "The Greatest Drama Ever Staged" with this perspective: "The Christian faith is the most exciting drama that ever staggered the imagination of man. . . .The plot pivots upon a single character, and the whole action is the answer to a single central problem: *What think ye of Christ?*"[1] It is an apt assessment and, since Sayers was a classicist, a Christian, and a dramatist, it is one which classical Christian schools should deeply ponder.

Is Drama Mentioned in the Bible?

The Bible does not directly mention drama or theatrical performances primarily because in Jewish culture of the earliest times, stage representations were considered a form of idolatry.

When the campaigns of Alexander the Great brought Greek culture into the region of the Israelites, the culture became Hellenized, that is to say, it was influenced by Greek (Hellenic) civilization, which, of course, included theatres. Because of the pagan origin and purpose of the early performances, which were meant to honor pagan gods, the Jews continued to have little to do with them. However, over time, Hellenized Jews began attending the theatre and eventually began to use drama to present Biblical narratives.

One of the first to do so was a man by the name of Ezekiel, who lived in Alexandria. In the second century BC, Ezekiel wrote a play called *Exagoge*, which tells the story of Moses. Jewish theatre director Yoni Oppenheim believes that works such as Ezekiel's "probably served a political purpose in allowing Jews to present themselves as a law-abiding people with a philosophical understanding of God, at a time when the persecution of Jews was an emerging threat."[2]

Yet, despite the fact that the word *theatre* does not appear in the Bible, the Jews did

Dance of Miriam from Exodus 15

employ the tools of drama (dialogue and music) in order to express themselves. Take, for example, the narrative of the Red Sea crossing in Exodus 20. Moses' song, Miriam's music and dance, and the musical response of the Hebrew women have distinct dramatic elements. Says the Jewish scholar Max Seligsohn, "Miriam with a drum in her hand, singing the deliverance of Israel, while the other women answer her in chorus, suggests vividly the strophes and antistrophes of the later Greek."[3]

Seligsohn points to other dramatic narratives in the Old Testament as well, identifying the Song of Solomon as "a regular drama, the heroine of which is the Shulamite, and in which the other *dramatis personae* are: Solomon; a shepherd; chorus, watchmen, etc." He viewed the Book of Job similarly, noting "if not so elaborate in dramatic form as the Canticles, [it] yet represents several persons as acting: namely, Job; his wife; the messengers; Eliphaz, Bildad, and Zophar (Job's three friends); Elihu, and God.[4]

There is another way in which Bible narratives have a dramatic purpose. Shakespeare, through the voice of Hamlet, said that the purpose of theatre:

> . . . both at the
> first and now, was and is, to hold, as 'twere, the
> mirror up to nature; to show virtue her own feature,
> scorn her own image, and the very age and body of
> the time his form and pressure (*Ham.* 3.2).

In short, there is a moral purpose to drama: to "hold the mirror up" so that humans can see themselves in the dramatic action before them and learn to recognize "virtue" and "scorn" those actions in themselves that do not comport with it. This purpose is readily seen in the Old Testament narrative in which Nathan rebukes David by presenting him with a mini-drama. It proceeds in this manner:

Nathan Rebukes David

The LORD sent Nathan to David. When he came to him, he said, "There were two men in a certain town, one rich and the other poor. The rich man had a very large number of sheep and cattle, but the poor man had nothing except one little ewe lamb he had bought. He raised it, and it grew up with him and his children. It shared his food, drank from his cup and even slept in his arms. It was like a daughter to him.

The prophet Nathan rebukes David

"Now a traveler came to the rich man, but the rich man refrained from taking one of his own sheep or cattle to prepare a meal for the traveler who had come to him. Instead, he took the ewe lamb that belonged to the poor man and prepared it for the one who had come to him."

David burned with anger against the man and said to Nathan, "As surely as the LORD lives, the man who did this must die! He must pay for that lamb four times over, because he did such a thing and had no pity."

Then Nathan said to David, "You are the man!" (2 Samuel 12:1-7a)

What has Nathan done here? He has told David a story—we might call it an allegory or a parable—which clearly presented the choice between good and evil. He has elicited from David, his audience, a response to the injustice perpetrated by the rich man, and once David has become fully committed, Nathan drives home the point: "You are the man!" Nathan then goes on, showing David the injustice he has inflicted on Uriah by his double sin: killing Uriah and taking his wife, Bathsheba, for himself. When Nathan has finished, David responds: "I have sinned against the Lord." He has looked in the mirror that Nathan held up, and he has, indeed, seen himself and confessed his sin.

In the New Testament as well, we see the dramas of the nativity story, the crucifixion and resurrection, and the ascension. The book of Acts is a concatenation of vignettes that reveal the dramatic experiences of the early Christians, and Revelation is, in one sense, a drama that God allows to unfold in the sky, providing the apostle John the material for his narrative of the end times. The word *gospel* itself, which is derived from the Old English *godspell,* meaning "good story," reveals the dramatic nature of the New Testament story, and many a listener has been held *spellbound* during its telling. It is, indeed, as many have said through the centuries, "the greatest story ever told."

Why Drama at a Classical School?

Quintilian (c. AD 35 – c. AD 100)

In his *Institutes of Oratory*, Quintilian, citing Cato the Elder, argued that the purpose of education was to produce *vir bonus dicendi peritus*—that is, a good man speaking well (12.1.1). This famous statement presents a two-pronged approach: the development of ethics and morals, on the one hand, and the ability to present ideas proficiently, on the other. This two-pronged approach is directly related to the drama curriculum of a classical Christian school. It prepares students to weigh ideas, approach plays through the Judeo-Christian worldview, and present them in a way that wins the hearts and minds of the audience. It is a gargantuan task, but a necessary—and enjoyable—one.

Classical schools, we often explain, are based on the classical *trivium,* and if we recall that the word *trivium* is Latin for "three ways" of approaching the liberal arts— grammar, logic, and rhetoric—and combine with that the fourth component of the *quadrivium*—music—we see the way forward for the director of the drama classes and the school play in a classical school.

Grammar Stage

At the grammar stage in a drama class, students begin by learning such things as theatre terminology, the history of the theatre, the dramatic genres, the names of some of the classic dramatists, and the arguments (synopses) of some of the great plays. They also learn such features of theatre as the characters (*protagonist* and *antagonist*) and the parts of a play (rising action, climax, denouement). They might learn techniques of stage combat. If a dialect or accent is required for a certain character, they might work with a coach. The students practice inflection and projection of the voice. They learn the parts of the stage and basic stage directions. They memorize noted passages from famous plays.

Logic Stage

At the logic stage, students seek to understand the idea of the play (or its Thought, as Aristotle called it). This perspective then guides them in the interpretation of their characters. They discuss and debate the setting of the play (e.g., a war, the Roaring Twenties, etc.) and how the setting would shape the experiences of the characters and the way they think. They read and discuss classical plays. They view plays and discuss the director's vision for the portrayal of the piece. They play theatre games to gain confidence performing in front of people. They make decisions about what tone of voice is best suited to the character and the idea. They move toward the rhetoric stage by improvisational acting, employing gesture, motion, and voice to present short skits to one another. They experiment with stage makeup and costumes. They might learn how to create special effects with the use of the theatre lights. They build sets and work backstage.

Plato's Academy

Trivium: Rhetoric Stage

In theatre, the rhetoric stage is expressed, of course, in the final performance before a hushed audience. Makeup, costumes, sets, props, lights, music, and action—all come together to create a memorable theatre experience for the audience. In a kind of partnership with the audience, student actors project the personality of their characters throughout the auditorium. They raise laughter, applause, and an occasional sigh or gasp. They leave the audience feeling they have seen themselves in the various situations which, as human beings, they all face, and through the action, characters, and idea of the play, provide perspective on the proper path forward.

Quadrivium: Music

We tend to think of Socrates as we see him in the famous sculpture—bald, bearded, and grandfatherly. But it is also pleasing to recall that, as a teenager enrolled in a music school at Athens, he was handsome enough and talented enough to be selected to perform at the famous City Dionysius, the great festival of theatre and music in ancient Greece.

The importance of music to the education of the young was outlined by Plato in *The Republic,* where he wrote the following:

Musical training is a more potent instrument than any other, because rhythm and harmony find their way into the inward places of the soul, on which they mightily fasten, imparting grace, and making the soul of him who is rightly educated graceful, or of him who is ill-educated ungraceful; and also because he who has received this true education of the inner being will most shrewdly perceive omissions or faults in art and nature, and with a true taste, while he praises and rejoices over and receives into his soul the good, and becomes noble and good, he will justly blame and hate the bad, now in the days of his youth, even before he is able to know the reason why; and when reason comes he will recognize and salute the friend with whom his education has made him long familiar.[5]

Though the Broadway musicals of the twentieth century do not always have the acclaim of more serious dramas, their songs have become a part of the fabric of the nation, and some musicals have reached the status of classics: *The Sound of Music, Oliver!,* and *West Side Story,* among them. What is more, musicals provide an adaptation for the classical *prosopopoeia* (speech-in-character), which in earlier ages would have been presented in the soliloquy or monologue of the classic playwrights. Guinevere's "Simple Joys of Maidenhood" and Lancelot's "C'est Moi" from *Camelot,* for example, fit music to character in a delightful way, introducing the characters to the audience by allowing a peek into the their private thoughts in their first appearance on the stage.

Drama and Oratory

Before the revival of classical education in the twenty-first century, many would have associated the study of rhetoric with a composition class, but in antiquity it was primarily associated with oratory. No doubt, this was due in large part to the lack of a printing press or a steady supply of inexpensive paper, but even when books came along, oratory was considered a higher form of expression than mere writing, which did not employ the whole person—gesture, motion, and voice.

We must also remember that oratory, which Quintilian defined as "the art of persuading," was paramount in the foundation of democracy, which began, of course, in Athens. Since democracy involves debating, persuading, and voting, the Greek educators were charged with developing oratory in their students. After all, it was the *sine qua non* for the success of the jurist or Senator—or indeed of any citizen who had the right to argue for or against a law in the Senate.

Cicero (106 BC – 43 BC)

So how did the rhetoric teachers go about preparing their students for this role? The answer is that, in part, they directed their students to the study of actors.

In his treatise *On the Orator*, Cicero frequently compared the oral delivery of a jurist or Senator to that of an actor, asking his students: "And why need I add any remarks on delivery itself, which is to be ordered by action of body, by gesture, by look, and by modulation and variation of the voice, the great power of which, alone and in itself, the comparatively trivial art of actors and the stage proves . . . ?"[6]

In fact, when Cicero's "characters" Crassus and Antonius debate the art of speaking in *On the Orator*, Crassus refers so frequently to actors, and especially to the stunning comic actor Roscius, that Antonius laments: "You would have every one of us a Roscius in our profession!"[7]

"Well, yes," Crassus might have said. "Otherwise, how will you keep your audience awake long enough to persuade them to your side?" (My apologies to Cicero for this brash addition to his text.)

Therefore, since one of the goals of a classical education is to produce students who are prepared to hold sway in the marketplace of ideas, it follows that teaching students the dramatic arts prepares them for oratory. Drama class and school plays comport well with the goals and curriculum of classical education.

Why Drama in a Christian School?

The Great Commission

Russian icon depicting Mark the Evangelist

Mark, a disciple of Christ, records that at the end of Jesus' earthly ministry and just before he ascended into heaven, Jesus gave his followers this command: "Go into all the world and proclaim the gospel to the whole creation" (Mark 16:15). This statement has come to be called the Great Commission.

Linguistically, this last utterance of Jesus is in the imperative form; that is to say, it is a command. The subject is the understood *you*, which, we can see more easily in the King James translation to be plural. The command is not to be translated as "*Hie thee* into all the world," but rather "*Go ye* [all of you] . . . ." In short, every believer is to convey the gospel message to "the *whole* creation." Like Mark, Matthew also spoke of the Great Commission, indicating in his gospel that the end will not come until that commission is complete (24:14). More than 2,000 years later the Commission is still ongoing, and those in our generation are as equally charged as were our spiritual ancestors.

Now, in order to make the completion of the task possible, the Lord equips every believer with gifts that will further the mission of the Church, and, in the context of the Great Commission, the gift of communication is a considerable spiritual gift. Peter specifically named this gift, saying:

> As each has received a gift, use it to serve one another, as good stewards of God's varied grace: whoever speaks, as one who speaks oracles of God; whoever serves, as one who serves by the strength that God supplies—in order that in everything God may be glorified through Jesus Christ. To him belong glory and dominion forever and ever. Amen" (I Pet. 4:10-11).

We live in a time of moral and spiritual decline, and Broadway and Hollywood have earned themselves a reputation for immorality, but this was exactly the environment in which the Christian church emerged in the Roman Empire. Although the theatre of the time was in such a degraded state that both Christians *and* pagans covered it with invective, by the Middle Ages the Church was realizing the value of liturgical drama, which, of course, could be one way to fulfill the Great Commission. Over time, religious drama has expanded, and in our own age there have been efforts via stage, radio, movies, and TV to bring the gospel message to the world. Though not all have met with uncritical acclaim, they include well-intentioned works such as the radio drama *The Man Born to Be King* (Dorothy L. Sayers, 1941-42); the musical *Godspell* (John Michael Tebelak and Stephen Schwartz, 1971); and the movie *The Passion of the Christ* (Mel Gibson, 2004).

Judeo-Christian History

In addition to taking the gospel message to every generation, the theatrical community has used stage and film to convey events from Judeo-Christian history. One example is T. S. Eliot's stage play *Murder in the Cathedral* (1935), which dramatized the twelfth-century Church-state conflict that led to the assassination of Thomas Becket, Archbishop of Canterbury, and which was first performed in Canterbury Cathedral, where the murder had taken place in 1170. Another is the movie *Quo Vadis?* (1951), which concerned the persecution of Christians in the Roman Empire. Yet another is *Fiddler on the Roof* (1964), which recounted the persecution of the Jews in Russia in 1905.

Thirteenth-century depiction of the murder of Archbishop Thomas Becket

Biblical Worldview

Furthermore, beyond religious drama and history-based productions, numerous plays imparting Biblical values have emerged in predominantly Christian cultures. Take, for example, *My Fair Lady* (1956), which supports human equality and the institution of marriage; *Death of a Salesman* (1949), which shows what happens to a family when the father steps off the straight and narrow; and *Oklahoma!* (1943), which deals with the issues of chastity and godly manhood.

Othello and Desdemona in Venice

Even the Greek playwrights, living in pre-Christian times, found their way to universal truths in plays like *Antigone*, which concerned obedience to higher law; *Electra*, which showed the appalling ramifications of infidelity; and *The Persians*, which explored the sin of hubris. And in the Renaissance period, William Shakespeare showed his deep understanding of Jeremiah 17:9, "The heart is deceitful above all things and desperately wicked. Who can know it?" He depicted the destructive power of sin in the great tragedies: jealousy in *Othello*; ingratitude in *King Lear;* and unbridled ambition in *Macbeth*. Even his history plays dealt with weighty spiritual issues. For example, in *Henry V,* he focused on whether a soldier is accountable for his sin if he is just "following orders." In the *Henry IV* series, he presented the follies of misspent youth in the character of Prince Hal. And, like Shakespeare, his contemporary, Christopher Marlowe, explored the dreadful consequences of homosexuality and favoritism in his play entitled *Edward II.*

In short, theatre is, and long has been, a remarkable tool for reaching the world for Christ and carrying the Biblical worldview into the post-modern world.

In the Image of a Creative God

As one of the fine arts, theatre is an enterprise steeped in creativity, an attribute specifically assigned to mankind, as we are told in the first chapter of Genesis: "So God created man in his own image, in the image of God he created him; male and female he created them" (1:27). The arts involved in a dramatic production are numerous: costuming, stage make-up, set construction and painting, music, dance, and the artful use of stage lighting. Students can even choreograph plays and manage the sound system artfully. And, of course, the actors themselves express creativity in the way they present characters and portray mood, motive, and consequences.

Joyful Noise

In the movie *Chariots of Fire*, Eric Liddell explains to his sister that he has not forgotten the great purpose of his life in Christian missions but that he has also been blessed with great athletic skills: "I believe God made me for a purpose, but he also made me fast. And when I run, I feel His pleasure." What makes this line so memorable is that, even though we are all gifted in different ways, when we turn the talents he gave us into his service, he rewards us with joy: "The Lord your God will bless you in all your produce and in all the work of your hands, so that you will be altogether joyful" (Deut. 16:15).

Aristotle noted in his *Poetics* that joy was, in fact, the first cause of poetry (by which he meant playwriting): "The instinct of imitation is implanted in man from childhood, one difference between him and other animals being that he is the most imitative of living creatures, and through imitation learns his earliest lessons; and no less universal is the pleasure felt in things imitated."[8] Or, to put it in today's vernacular, it is just plain fun to get up a costume. Just putting on some cowboy boots, a cowboy hat, and a bandana can ignite the imagination of a five-year-old. And what teenager does not enjoy Spirit Week at school when each day brings a new theme and a new costume?

In drama class, joy comes from the camaraderie that is built among the cast and crew, from the encouragement of parents, from the applause at the end of the performance, and from the satisfaction of a job well done. Like playing sports, performing on stage can be exhilarating, and when we perform in a way that honors the Lord, we do indeed "feel His pleasure."

A student performance of *Beauty and the Beast*

Summing Up

Perhaps the best way to close a discussion about the ways in which theatre arts support the Christian mission is with this statement from the University of Mary Hardin-Baylor, a Christian university in Belton, Texas. The school's College of Visual and Performing Arts expresses it this way:

> God-glorifying arts can be realistic or fantastic, representational or symbolic or abstract. Artistic creativity and beauty are the gifts of God. Their function is to glorify God and refresh people. Like other gifts, they can be misused and redirected from their God-given purpose. The biblical perspective toward the arts, therefore, steers artistic expression and creativity toward ultimate truth, beauty, and goodness.[9]

Truth, Beauty, and Goodness—Christianity's link to the classical virtues: *Veritas, Decorum, Bonitas*—dramatic performance achieves the highest goals of both classical and Christian education.

B. Board Idea

EXERCISE 1.1: Discussion Questions

Directions: To reflect on some of the issues raised in this chapter, please discuss the following questions with your classmates.

1. Tell about a time when you had fun dressing up or wearing a costume when you were a child. What was your costume? How did you put it together? How did you feel when you put it on?

2. How did you turn household items into props or costumes in a game of make-believe with your friends? For example, did you ever turn a pillow case into a cape? How about using a stick as a sword?

3. If you have ever performed in a musical, share with your classmates a song that works like a speech-in-character to show the character's thoughts and personality.

4. Name some plays or movies that resolved a play's conflict in a manner that would accord with Scriptural teaching (like the example of support for marriage in *My Fair Lady*).

5. Offer your thoughts on any religious dramas in which you have participated or which you have seen. What ideas and/or narratives did they communicate? Did they accord with or depart from Scripture?

6. What position does your church hold with respect to the stage portrayal of Christ or members of the Holy Family? Can nativity plays at Christmas and passion plays at Easter be considered a form of idolatry? Explain your thoughts.

Christian Students in the Drama Class

In Paul's second epistles to the Corinthians, he wrote, "We . . . take every thought captive to obey Christ" (10:5b). This statement has important ramifications for the Christian actor. For one thing, when one is examining the heart of an evil character, such as Lady Macbeth in Shakespeare's famous play, it is important to know where one's own personality ends and the character's begins. Scripture has made it clear: "Be sober-minded; be watchful. Your adversary the devil prowls around like a roaring lion, seeking someone to devour. Resist him" (I Pet. 5:8-9a).

Probably the most stark example of what can happen when an actor identifies too closely with a character is the story of Australian actor Heath Ledger. On November 28, 2007, an entertainment feature appeared on *Yahoo! UK & Ireland* stating that, in order to prepare for his role as the Joker in the forthcoming blockbuster movie, *The Dark Knight*, Australian actor Heath Ledger had "locked himself away for a month while he perfected the maniac laugh,"[10] a key feature of the villain of the Batman legend. The article went on to say that Ledger had "gone all out" in his preparation for the character: He told *Empire* magazine:

> It's a combination of reading all the comic books I could that were relevant to the script and then just closing my eyes and meditating on it. . . . I sat around in a hotel room in London for about a month, locked myself away, formed a little diary and experimented with voices — it was important to try to find a somewhat iconic voice and laugh. I ended up landing more in the realm of a psychopath — someone with very little to no conscience towards his acts. He's just an absolute sociopath, a cold-blooded, mass-murdering clown, and Chris [Nolan, the director] has given me free rein. Which is fun, because there

are no real boundaries to what The Joker [*sic*] would say or do. Nothing intimidates him, and everything is a big joke.[11]

The piece then concluded with what seemed just two months later to be an ominous clincher: "We can't wait," the author said, "to see (and hear) the finished results"—ominous because on January 22, 2008, Heath Ledger died as the result of an accidental overdose of prescription painkillers, anti-anxiety meds, and sleeping pills that he had taken to drive out the nightmares and anxiety which had plagued him in the weeks following the making of *The Dark Knight*. Had the writer of the November 2007 article known what was going to happen, he or she might not have entitled the piece, "Ledger Went Bat Crazy Preparing for Joker Role"—funny in 2007, but insensitive and heartbreaking now.[1]

Though total immersion in a character is perhaps the most serious danger for an actor, there are other spiritual considerations for Christian actors. For example, Christian actors must be careful to put their sense of worth not in their own performance, but in Christ. Some actors have been known to put their fist through a wall after a performance did not go well, but since self-control is one of the fruits of the Spirit, Christian actors are well prepared to put things into perspective, realizing that, like athletes, the quality of their performance will vary from time to time.

Another pull that needs to be surrendered to Christ is that of rancorous competition among students for various roles. In and of itself, competition is not bad. Paul, after all, was a runner who understood the purpose of competition and even encouraged the disciples to run for the prize, which, in this case, was the winning of souls:

> Do you not know that in a race all the runners run, but only one receives the prize? So run that you may obtain it (1 Cor. 9:24).

But Paul did not stop there. He continued with this note of caution:

> Every athlete exercises self-control in all things. They do it to receive a perishable wreath, but we an imperishable. I do not run aimlessly; I do not box

---

[1] Update May 2016: The line "We can't wait. . . ." has since been removed from the Internet article.

as one beating the air. But I discipline my body and keep it under control, lest after preaching to others, I myself should be disqualified (9:25-27)

The application of this teaching to theatrical competition is twofold: (a) one can compete strongly in order to win the desired role, but (b) one must remember that it is, after all, *only* a role that one plays for a season (i.e., it is "perishable"). Like athletes, the Christian actors must exercise self-control in all things, acknowledging the talents of others and praising the Lord in all circumstances (I Thess. 5:18).

Last, there might be roles that a Christian actor will need to turn down. Before accepting a role, one should know what behavior is going to be expected of the character and, of necessity, therefore, by the actor. In this respect, one might ask, "Is this a role my parents would be happy to see me play?" Drama teachers in Christian schools can normally be counted on to select wholesome plays, but students are advised to read the whole play before accepting a part and to be ready to say no if, as a follower of Christ, they do not consider the play appropriate. Once again, Paul provides a benchmark:

> Finally, brothers, whatever is true, whatever is honorable, whatever is just, whatever is pure, whatever is lovely, whatever is commendable, if there is any excellence, if there is anything worthy of praise, think about these things (Phil. 4:8).

EXERCISE 1.2: For Discussion

Directions: With your classmates, discuss these issues related to moral and ethical matters as they relate to theatre production.

1. Have you ever known a person who "got lost" in a character either in drama or a role-playing game? If so, without providing names, describe the circumstances to your classmates

2. Are there any roles which, as a Christian, you would feel obligated to turn down?

3. Under what circumstances might you be willing to play the role of an evil character in a play?

THEATRE BASICS

Chapter 2

Basic Theatre Language

Persons

Producer—the person in charge of hiring the director, establishing the budget and finding investors

Director—the person in charge of all aspects of the production

Scenic Designer—the person in charge of the overall theme of the play; works with all backstage crews to effect the director's vision

Business Manager—the person in charge of the receipts and daily expenditures of a production

Technical Director—the person in charge of all of the crews (costumes, set, lighting, etc.); makes sure the scenic designer's vision is executed

Musical Director—the person in charge of teaching the music to the actors and directing the orchestra in a musical

Choreographer—the person in charge of creating and teaching the dancing and movement in a musical

Assistant Director—the person who serves as an assistant to the director and is the liaison between the director and the cast and crew

House Manager—the person in charge of the box office (where the tickets are sold), ushering, and all of the needs of the audience

Publicity Manager—the person in charge of advertising the production

Stage Manager—the person in charge of the actors; keeps them on schedule, feeds them their lines, assists the director in rehearsals, and calls the cues during performances

Costume Designer—the person in charge of designing, creating or securing all of the clothing that the actors wear onstage; makes sure the costumes accurately represent the time period, locale, and overall theme of the production

Properties Chief—the person in charge of securing all physical items (props) needed for the show

Lighting Designer—the person who creates the theme of the production using lighting, color, and design elements; signals scene changes turning out the stage lights

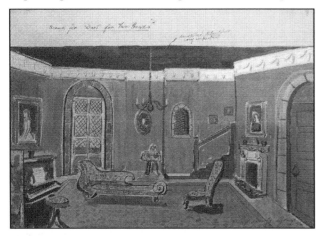

Set design for *Duet for Two Hands* by Reginald Gray

Sound Designer—the person who creates the theme of the production using sound cues; manages microphones used for the actors; balances with the orchestra

Stage Hands / Grips—the people who move the scenery and props onstage; wear black clothing so that they will not be seen while moving scenery

Critic—a person who attends the performance and gives a written or verbal critique of the overall production usually to a news outlet

Cast—the actors in the production

Crew—the people who work on all of the technical and backstage elements of the production (sets, costumes, lights, backstage area, etc.)

Company—the entire group of people working on the show, including the directors, cast and crew

Parts of the Stage

House—the name of the physical structure of the theatre as a whole

Backstage or Back of the House—that is behind the main acting area

Dressing Room—the room where the actors prepare their hair, makeup and costumes for the show

Green Room—the room where the actors can relax and wait when they are not needed onstage. (NOTE: Today most green rooms are not actually green in color. It is believed that perhaps the earliest waiting area was green, and the term "green room" simply persisted)

Front of the House—the area where the audience enters and where they sit

Box Office—the area where the tickets are sold before the show; so named because originally the money taken in was placed in a simple box

Stage—the area where the actors perform

Proscenium Arch—the structure (not necessarily shaped like an arch) which serves to "frame" the stage (see Fig. 1).

Proscenium Arch

Apron—a section of the stage that extends forward in front of the main curtain

Fly—the area above the stage

Wings—the areas at the sides of the stage where actors wait to go onstage and where props and set pieces can be stored

Fourth Wall—an imaginary wall between the audience and the actors in a representational play

Sight Lines—lines indicating visibility of onstage and backstage areas from various points in the house

Orchestra Pit—a lowered area between the stage and the audience where the orchestra plays during a performance

Orchestra Seating—the seats closest to the stage

Mezzanine—the seats behind the orchestra seating, the second tier

Balcony—the seats in the third tier, upstairs

The Orchestra Pit by Everett Shinn (1876-1953).

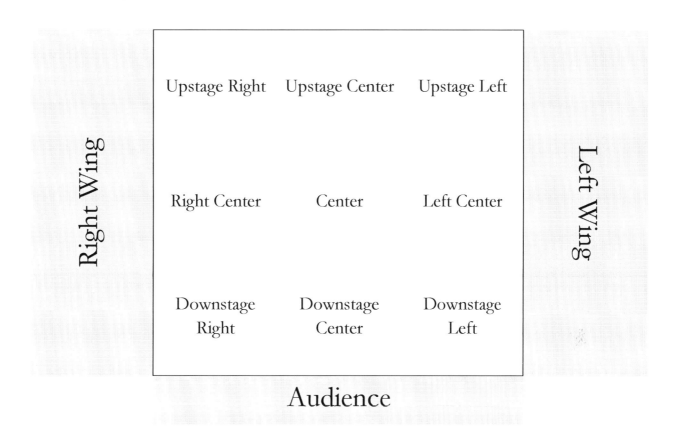

Figure 1: Diagram of Stage Directions

Stage Directions

Center Stage—the position in the center of the stage, as the actor faces the audience

Stage Right—the area to the right of an actor who is facing the audience

Stage Left—the area to the left of an actor who is facing the audience

Upstage—the direction the actor takes when moving away from the audience (NOTE: The earliest stages sloped toward the audience, so actors would literally move "up" when moving away or "down" when moving toward the audience.)

Downstage—the direction the actor moves when moving toward the audience

Audience Right/Left—the area to the right or left of the audience members as they view the stage

Closed Position—the position of the actor who is turned away from the audience (NOTE: When at all possible, an actor never turns his or her back to the audience.)

Same Plane—the position which makes one actor parallel to another when they are delivering their lines, preventing the necessity for either actor to turn his or her back to the audience

To Open Up—to take a position that assures the actor actually faces the audience

To Cheat—to adopt an onstage body position that is perhaps more open than one would adopt in reality; taken to ensure that the audience has a good view of the actor

To Counter—To fill the place left by another actor who has just crossed the stage

Types of Theatres

Arena / Amphitheatre/ Stadium / Theatre-in-the-Round—a theatre in which the audience sits on all four sides of the stage

Thrust Stage at the Pasant Theatre, Michigan State University

Thrust Stage—a theatre configuration in which the audience sits on three sides of the stage

Proscenium Theatre—a theatre arrangement in which the audience sits on one side of the stage, and the stage is framed by a proscenium arch

Raked Stage—a stage that slopes upward, thus elevating actors who are upstage

Black Box Theatre—a large square room with a flat floor in which the performance space is unadorned; often used for experimental productions

Characters and Actors

Antagonist—the villain

Protagonist—the hero or heroine

Chorus / Townsperson / Ensemble—actors who are a part of the cast but are not principal characters; they may or may not have speaking lines or solos but are vital to the overall setting of the show.

Bit Part—an acting role with very few lines

Principals—the main characters in a play or the named characters in a musical

Supporting Role—an acting role secondary to the lead role

Performance Terms

Audition—an interview-like opportunity in which actors are able to demonstrate their talents, meet the person hiring the cast, and make their first impression; used as a noun ("Auditions are tomorrow") or a verb ("We audition on Friday.")

Callback—an invitation to an actor to return for a second audition ("Hey, Mom, I got a callback!")

Irving Berlin, Richard Rodgers, Oscar Hammerstein II, and Helen Tamiris watching auditions at the St. James Theatre

Blocking—the movement onstage designed by the director for the actor ("We haven't blocked the scene yet.")

Marking Out—placing marks on the stage floor (usually with masking tape) to indicate the location of sets and large props, like furniture; usually done by the stage manager

Rehearsal—the time when actors prepare for the performance with the director

Call Time—the time an actor is supposed to be at the theatre to rehearse or perform; usually posted on a call board outside the theatre

Cue—a signal for the actor to enter, talk, or perform another action; can be verbal, nonverbal, or technical ("I forgot to give Veronica her cue.")

Cue to Cue—a process in which the actors and crew go through the beginning and end of each scene (without reciting any lines) in order to perfect the lighting and sound cues that begin and end each scene; usually done during tech week

Cue to Cue with Lines—a process in which actors run through their lines as fast as they can with the other actors, employing neither blocking nor voice inflection in order to facilitate memorization and tighten up scenes that are dragging

Tech Week—the week before the first performance, a time when all of the technical elements of the show come together (costumes, set, lights, props, hair, and make-up)

Running the Show—rehearsing the show in its entirety with or without the technical elements

Dress Rehearsal—a rehearsal of the show with costumes and all of the technical elements, usually done during tech week

Black Out—term used to describe time between scenes or at the end of an act when the stage lights are off and/or the curtain is closed

Striking the Set—taking down the set

Matinee—an afternoon performance

Dark—a term used to describe the theatre when no performances are being given ("The theatre is dark this week.")

"Break a leg!"—what actors say to each other to offer their wish for a successful performance (NOTE: It is considered "bad luck" to say "good luck" in a theatre, so actors adopted the saying "Break a leg" instead. The term is associated with the way the knee "breaks" when curtseying or giving a stage bow to the audience.)

Intermission—a 15-minute break in the middle of a show

Curtain Call—a term that designates the time at the end of a show when the actors bow to the audience and receive applause

Curtain call at Don Giovanni Opera, Australia 2014

Parts of a Play

Exposition—the introduction of character, setting, background information, and conflict

Rising Action—events in which the characters try to resolve the conflict

Climax—the tense moment which determines the outcome

Falling Action—those events that are a direct result of the climax

Denouement—[dā-nū-MÄ]—the point at which loose ends are tied, mysteries are cleared up, conflicts are solved

Acting Terms

Cold reading—performing a scene from a script one has never seen before ("Your cold reading of Richard III's monologue was excellent" or "I read it cold.")

Improvisation—a form of live theatre in which the plot, characters, and dialogue of a game, scene, or story are made up in the moment

Beat—a pause in the dialogue indicating the moment in a scene when a shift in emotion or topic occurs ("Add a beat after that line, Joseph.")

Articulation—clear and precise pronunciation

The French mime Jyjou* in typical mime's positions inspired by Etienne Decroux's pantomime technique

Gesture—an expressive movement of the body or limbs

Inflection—variety in the tone of voice (for emphasis, etc.)

Pantomime—acting through facial expressions or gestures without words

Projecting—making one's voice fill the performance space

Feeding—giving lines and action in such a way that another character can make a point or get a laugh ("I fed him a line.")

Holding for Laughs—waiting for the audience to quiet down after a funny line or scene

Milking—drawing a maximum response from the audience from comic lines or action ("He really milked that line.")

Stealing a Scene—attracting attention to oneself onstage when it should rightfully go to another actor; considered bad manners in the theatrical community

Motivation—the underlying cause of a character's behavior ("What do you suppose is Hamlet's motivation for his strange behavior?")

Breaking Character—becoming oneself, instead of the character, on the stage; occurs by making unplanned eye contact with the audience, giggling, laughing, or muttering words to oneself or the audience during the performance

Breaking the Fourth Wall—breaking the illusion of the four walls of the setting by making eye contact with the audience (done on purpose when a script calls for an aside)

Ad libbing—making up words or actions, usually to cover a mistake in performance ("Veronica forgot her lines, but Jadon ad libbed so well no one noticed.")

Picking up Cues—reducing the amount of time between speeches and/or lines ("We need to pick up the cues a bit.")

Projecting—making sure one's performance is audible and visible from every seat in the house

Off book—rehearsing without a script ("Actors prepare to perform off book.")

Monologue—a long speech by a single character while other characters are also onstage

Soliloquy—a long speech by a single character while alone on the stage; intended to show the audience the character's inner thoughts and feelings

Lady Macbeth's soliloquy performed by Ellen Terry, 1889

Subtext—implied meanings behind dialogue either indicated in the script or interpreted by the actor ("You can tell from the subtext here that Hamlet is quite bitter.")

Calling for a Line—requesting a prompt when one has forgotten the lines ("Just say 'line,' and I'll give you a prompt.")

Upstaging an Actor—a phrase synonymous with *stealing the scene*; alternatively, being too far upstage from one's fellow actor, forcing the downstage actor to turn his or her back to the audience

"Show Biz" Terms

Broadway—New York City's principal theatre district

Off Broadway—a term for plays which are performed in theatres not in the principal theatre district

Royalties—fees paid to the copyright holder to have the right to produce a play

Actors' Equity Union—a labor union for actors, which preserves workers' rights regarding pay, break time, hours worked per week, etc.

Points—credits received for each performance one works on to be accumulated until the artist is eligible for the protection of the actors' union

Professional / Equity Status—status achieved by an actor who has received enough points to become a part of the Actors' Equity Union

Robert Cohen's "GOTE"

Robert Cohen, Chair of Drama at the University of California at Irvine, has devised a method by which actors can prepare to understand and represent the character they have been chosen to play. The method, now widely used, has come to be known by the acronym GOTE, which stands for "Goal, Obstacle, Tactics, and Expectation."

Robert Cohen

Goal

The term *goal* refers to what the character is trying to achieve. This can be the overall goal or the specific goal. Let's take the play *My Fair Lady* as an example. Eliza

Doolittle's overall goal is to achieve a better life for herself, and her specific goal is to improve her speech so that she can work in a flower shop.

Obstacle

The term *obstacle* refers to whatever is preventing the character from accomplishing the goal. In the case of Eliza Doolittle, lack of education, lower class social status, Cockney accent, her drunkard father, and, of course, the cold and impersonal nature of Professor Henry Higgins, who believes he can turn a lower-class person into a respectable member of society by changing the way in which the person speaks.

Eliza Doolittle as portrayed by Ingeborg von Kusserow

Tactics

The term *tactics* refers to the way the character goes about achieving his or her goal. For example, an actor might approach the problem boldly, shyly, aggressively, cheerily, or passionately. In *My Fair Lady*, Eliza boldly stands up to Henry Higgins (unusual for the time and place of the play) yet keeps a teachable spirit, patiently allowing herself to be molded by the professor in terms of speech and comportment.

Expectation

The term *expectation* describes the degree to which the character expects actually to achieve the desired goal. How the actor assesses the character's degree of optimism determines the way he or she will play the character going forward. By closely reading the script, an actress playing Eliza would normally perceive these actions: she leaves her home in the slums of London, takes up chaperoned residence in the professor's mansion, and works hard to better herself. These actions show that Eliza is fairly optimistic that Professor Higgins might be on to something. This understanding will help the actress show the audience just why it is that Eliza is willing to work fairly unflappably into the wee small hours of the morning.

One advantage of using the GOTE method is that actors can interpret the characters without investing their own personal emotions.

EXERCISE 2.1: Working with Stage Directions

Directions: Begin by appointing one student to be the "director" for this practice. Then divide into two teams. Designate the area in your classroom that will serve as a stage, and send one member of each team to that area. The "director," using the cues in Group A, will call out a position, such as, "Stage right!" The first competitor to reach that position wins a point for his or her team. As time goes on, you can call out more challenging commands by combining cues from Group A and Group B, such as, "Go downstage right and face profile left!"

GROUP A

Upstage right	Upstage center	Upstage left
Right center	Center	Left center
Downstage right	Downstage center	Downstage left

GROUP B

One-quarter position left	One quarter position right
Profile left	Profile right
Three-quarter position left	Three-quarter position right
Full front position	

EXERCISE 2.2: Practicing GOTE

Directions: Break up into small groups of three or four students. Choose a character from the list below or another with which you are familiar, and apply the GOTE method to help you understand the character in terms of goal, obstacle, tactics, and expectation.

a. Aslan in *The Lion, The Witch, and the Wardrobe*

b. Frodo in *Lord of the Rings*

c. Darth Vader in *Star Wars*

d. Dorothy in *The Wizard of Oz*

e. Katniss Everdeen *The Hunger Games*

EXERCISE 2.3: Being a Detective

<u>Directions</u>: Begin by reading the play "Campbell of Kilmohr" by J. A. Ferguson, which appears below. After reading the play, choose one character and answer the questions below which will help you analyze him or her. This activity is designed to help you understand any subtext that underlies the dialogue. If the script does not yield the information, make an educated decision. Leave nothing blank.

The Battle of Culloden, 1745, background of the play *Campbell of Kilmhor*

CAMPBELL OF KILMHOR
a play in one-act

by J.A. Ferguson

The following one-act play is reprinted from *The Atlantic Book of Modern Plays*. Ed. Sterling Andrus Leonard. Boston: Atlantic Monthly Press, 1921. It is now in the public domain and may therefore be performed without royalties.

CHARACTERS

MARY STEWART
MORAG CAMERON
DUGALD STEWART
CAPTAIN SANDEMAN
ARCHIBALD CAMPBELL
JAMES MACKENZIE

SETTING
Interior of a lonely cottage on the road from Struan to Rannoch
in North Perthshire.

TIME
After the Rising of 1745.

[MORAG is restlessly moving backwards and forwards. The old woman is seated on a low stool beside the peat fire in the centre of the floor.]

[The room is scantily furnished and the women are poorly clad. MORAG is barefooted. At the back is the door that leads to the outside. On the left of the door is a small window. On the right side of the room there is a door that opens into a barn. MORAG stands for a moment at the window, looking out.]

MORAG: It is the wild night outside.

MARY STEWART: Is the snow still coming down?

MORAG: It is that, then--dancing and swirling with the wind too, and never stopping at all. Aye, and so black I cannot see the other side of the road.

MARY STEWART: That is good.

[MORAG moves across the floor and stops irresolutely. She is restless, expectant.]

MORAG: Will I be putting the light in the window?

MARY STEWART: Why should you be doing that? You have not heard his call *(turns eagerly)*, have you?

MORAG: *(with sign of head)* No, but the light in the window would show him all is well.

MARY STEWART: It would not, then! The light was to be put there *after* we had heard the signal.

MORAG: But on a night like this he may have been calling for long and we never hear him.

MARY STEWART: Do not be so anxious, Morag. Keep to what he says. Put more peat on the fire now and sit down.

MORAG: *(with increasing excitement)* I canna, I canna! There is that in me that tells me something is going to befall us this night. Oh, that wind! Hear to it, sobbing round the house as if it brought some poor lost soul up to the door, and we refusing it shelter.

MARY STEWART: Do not be fretting yourself like that. Do as I bid you. Put more peats to the fire.

MORAG: *(at the wicker peat-basket)* Never since I.... What was that?

[Both listen for a moment.]

MARY STEWART: It was just the wind; it is rising more. A sore night for them that are out in the heather.

[MORAG puts peat on the fire without speaking.]

MARY STEWART: Did you notice were there many people going by to-day?

MORAG: No. After daybreak the redcoats came by from Struan; and there was no more till nine, when an old man like the Catechist from Killichonan passed. At four o'clock, just when the dark was falling, a horseman with a lad holding to the stirrup, and running fast, went by towards Rannoch.

MARY STEWART: But no more redcoats?

MORAG: *(shaking her head)* The road has been as quiet as the hills, and they as quiet as the grave. Do you think will he come?

MARY STEWART: Is it you think I have the gift, girl, that you ask me that? All I know is that it is five days since he was here for meat and drink for himself and for the others--five days and five nights, mind you; and little enough he took away; and those in hiding no' used to such sore lying, I'll be thinking. He must try to get through to-night. But that quietness, with no one to be seen from daylight till dark, I do not like it, Morag. They must know something. They must be watching.

[A sound is heard by both women. They stand listening.]

MARY STEWART: Haste you with the light, Morag.

MORAG: But it came from the back of the house--from the hillside.

MARY STEWART: Do as I tell you. The other side may be watched.

[A candle is lit and placed in the window. Girl goes hurrying to the door.]

MARY STEWART: Stop, stop! Would you be opening the door with a light like that shining from the house? A man would be seen against it in the doorway for a mile. And who knows what eyes may be watching? Put out the light now and cover the fire.

[*Room is reduced to semi-darkness, and the door unbarred. Someone enters.*]

MORAG: You are cold, Dugald!

[*STEWART, very exhausted, signs assent.*]

MORAG: And wet, oh, wet through and through!

STEWART: Erricht Brig was guarded, well guarded. I had to win across the water.

[*The old woman has now relit candle and taken away plaid from fire.*]

MARY STEWART: Erricht Brig--then--

STEWART: *(nods)* Yes--in a corrie, on the far side of Dearig, half-way up.

MARY STEWART: Himself is there then?

STEWART: Aye, and Keppoch as well, and another and a greater is with them.

MARY STEWART: Wheest! *(Glances at MORAG.)*

STEWART: Mother, is it that you can--

MARY STEWART: Yes, yes, Morag will bring out the food for ye to carry back. It is under the hay in the barn, well hid. Morag will bring it.--Go, Morag, and bring it.

[*MORAG enters other room or barn which opens on right.*]

STEWART: Mother, I wonder at ye; Morag would never tell--never.

MARY STEWART: Morag is only a lass yet. She has never been tried. And who knows what she might be made to tell.

STEWART: Well, well, it is no matter, for I was telling you where I left them, but not where I am to *find* them.

MARY STEWART: They are not where you said now?

STEWART: No; they left the corrie last night, and I am to find them *(whispers)* in a quiet part on Rannoch moor.

MARY STEWART: It is as well for a young lass not to be knowing. Do not tell her.

[*He sits down at table; the old woman ministers to his wants.*]

STEWART: A fire is a merry thing on a night like this; and a roof over the head is a great comfort.

MARY STEWART: Ye'll no' can stop the night?

STEWART: No. I must be many a mile from here before the day breaks on Ben Dearig.

[MORAG reënters.]

MORAG: It was hard to get through, Dugald?

STEWART: You may say that. I came down Erricht for three miles, and then when I reached low country I had to take to walking in the burns because of the snow that shows a man's steps and tells who he is to them that can read; and there's plenty can do that abroad, God knows.

MORAG: But none spied ye?

STEWART: Who can tell? Before dark came, from far up on the slopes of Dearig I saw soldiers about; and away towards the Rannoch Moor they were scattered all over the country like black flies on a white sheet. A wild cat or anything that couldna fly could never have got through. And men at every brig and ford and pass! I had to strike away up across the slopes again; and even so as I turned round the bend beyond Kilrain I ran straight into a sentry sheltering behind a great rock. But after that it was easy going.

MORAG: How could that be?

STEWART: Well, you see I took the boots off him, and then I had no need to mind who might see my steps in the snow.

MORAG: You took the boots off him!

STEWART: *(laughing)* I did that same. Does that puzzle your bonny head? How does a lad take the boots off a redcoat? Find out the answer, my lass, while I will be finishing my meat.

MORAG: Maybe he was asleep?

STEWART: Asleep! Asleep! Well, well, he sleeps sound enough now, with the ten toes of him pointed to the sky.

[The old woman has taken up dirk from table. She puts it down again. MORAG sees the action and pushes dirk away so that it rolls off the table and drops to the floor. She hides her face in her hands.]

MARY STEWART: Morag, bring in the kebbuck o' cheese. Now that all is well and safe it is we that will look after his comfort to-night. *(MORAG goes into barn.)*--I mind well her mother saying to me--it was one day in the black winter that she died, when the frost took the land in its grip and the birds fell stiff from the trees, and the deer came down and put their noses to the door--I mind well her saying just before she died--

[Loud knocking at the door.]

A VOICE: In the King's name!

[Both rise.]

MARY STEWART: The hay in the barn, quick, my son.

[Knocking continues.]

A VOICE: Open in the King's name!

[STEWART snatches up such articles as would reveal his presence and hurries into barn. He overlooks dirk on floor. The old woman goes towards door.]

MARY STEWART: Who is there? What do you want?

A VOICE: Open, open.

[MARY STEWART opens door and CAMPBELL OF KILMHOR follows CAPTAIN SANDEMAN into the house. Behind KILMHOR comes a man carrying a leather wallet, JAMES MACKENZIE, his clerk. The rear is brought up by soldiers carrying arms.]

SANDEMAN: Ha, the bird has flown.

CAMPBELL: *(who has struck dirk with his foot and picked it up)* But the nest is warm; look at this.

SANDEMAN: It seems as if we had disturbed him at supper. Search the house, men.

MARY STEWART: I'm just a lonely old woman. You have been misguided. I was getting through my supper.

CAMPBELL: *(holding up dirk)* And this was your toothpick, eh? Na! Na! We ken whaur we are, and wha we want, and by Cruachan, I think we've got him.

[Sounds are heard from barn, and soldiers return with MORAG. She has stayed in hiding from fear, and she still holds the cheese in her hands.]

SANDEMAN: What have we here?

CAMPBELL: A lass!

MARY STEWART: It's just my dead brother's daughter. She was getting me the cheese, as you can see.

CAMPBELL: On, men, again: the other turtle doo will no' be far away. *(Banteringly to the old woman)* Tut, tut, Mistress Stewart, and do ye have her wait upon ye while your leddyship dines alane! A grand way to treat your dead brother's daughter; fie, fie, upon ye!

[Soldiers reappear with STEWART, whose arms are pinioned.]

CAMPBELL: Did I no' tell ye! And this, Mrs. Stewart, will be your dead sister's son, I'm thinking; or aiblins your leddyship's butler! Weel, woman, I'll tell ye this: Pharaoh spared ae butler, but Erchie Campbell will no' spare anither. Na! na! Pharaoh's case is no' to be taken as forming ony preceedent. And so if he doesna answer certain questions we have to speir at him, before morning he'll hang as high as Haman.

[STEWART is placed before the table at which CAMPBELL has seated himself. Two soldiers guard STEWART. Another is behind CAMPBELL'S chair and another is by the door. The clerk, MACKENZIE, is seated at up corner of table. SANDEMAN stands by the fire.]

CAMPBELL: *(to STEWART)* Weel, sir, it is within the cognizance of the law that you have knowledge and information of the place of harbor and concealment used by certain persons who are in a state of proscription. Furthermore, it is known that four days ago certain other proscribed persons did join with these, and that they are banded together in an endeavor to secure the escape from these dominions of His Majesty, King George, of certain persons who by their crimes and treasons lie open to the capital charge. What say ye?

[STEWART makes no reply.]

CAMPBELL: Ye admit this then?

[STEWART as before.]

CAMPBELL: Come, come, my lad. Ye stand in great jeopardy. Great affairs of state lie behind this which are beyond your simple understanding. Speak up and it will be the better for ye.

[STEWART silent as before.]

CAMPBELL: Look you. I'll be frank with you. No harm will befall you this night--and I wish all in this house to note my words--no harm will befall you this night if you supply the information required.

[STEWART as before.]

CAMPBELL: *(with sudden passion)* Sandeman, put your sword to the carcass o' this muckle ass and see will it louse his tongue.

STEWART: It may be as well then, Mr. Campbell, that I should say a word to save your breath. It is this: Till you talk Rannoch Loch to the top of Schiehallion, ye'll no' talk me into a yea or nay.

CAMPBELL: *(quietly)* Say ye so? Noo, I widna be so very sure if I were you. I've had a lairge experience o' life, and speaking out of it I would say that only fools and the dead never change their minds.

STEWART: *(quietly too)* Then you'll be adding to your experience to-night, Mr. Campbell, and you'll have something to put on to the other side of it.

CAMPBELL: *(tapping his snuff-box)* Very possibly, young sir, but what I would present for your consideration is this: While ye may be prepared to keep your mouth shut under the condition of a fool, are ye equally prepared to do so in the condition of a dead man?

[CAMPBELL waits expectantly. STEWART silent as before.]

CAMPBELL: Tut, tut, now, if it's afraid ye are, my lad, with my hand on my heart and on my word as a gentleman--

STEWART: Afraid!

[He spits in contempt towards CAMPBELL.]

CAMPBELL: *(enraged)* Ye stubborn Hieland stot. *(To SANDEMAN)* Have him taken out. We'll get it another way.

[CAMPBELL rises. STEWART is moved into barn by soldiers.]

CAMPBELL: *(walking)* Some puling eediots, Sandeman, would applaud this contumacy and call it constancy. Constancy! Now, I've had a lairge experience o' life, and I never saw yet a sensible man insensible to the touch of yellow metal. If there may be such aman, it is demonstrable that he is no sensible man. Fideelity! quotha, it's sheer obstinacy. They just see that ye want something oot o' them, and they're so selfish and thrawn they winna pairt. And with the natural inabeelity o' their brains to hold mair than one idea at a time they canna see that in return you could put something into their palms far more profitable. *(Sits again at table.)* Aweel, bring Mistress Stewart up.

[Old woman is placed before him where son had been.]

CAMPBELL: *(more ingratiatingly)* Weel noo, Mistress Stewart, good woman, this is a sair predeecament for ye to be in. I would jist counsel ye to be candid. Doubtless yer mind is a' in a swirl. Ye kenna what way to turn. Maybe ye are like the Psalmist and say:"I lookit this way and that, and there was no man to peety me, or to have compassion upon my fatherless children." But, see now, ye would be wrong; and, if ye tell me a' ye ken, I'll stand freends wi' ye. Put your trust in Erchie Campbell.

MARY STEWART: I trust no Campbell.

CAMPBELL: Weel, weel noo, I'm no' jist that set up wi' them myself. There's but ae Campbell that I care muckle aboot, after a'. But, good wife, it's no' the Campbells we're trying the noo; so as time presses we'll jist *"birze yont,"* as they say themselves. Noo then, speak up.

[MARY STEWART is silent.]

CAMPBELL: *(beginning grimly and passing through astonishment, expostulation, and a feigned contempt for mother and pity for son, to a pretence of sadness which, except at the end, makes his words come haltingly)* Ah! ye also. I suppose ye understand, woman, how it will go wi' your son? *(To his clerk)* Here's a fine mother for ye, James! Would you believe it? She kens what would save her son--the very babe she once sang to sleep; but will she save him? Na! na! Sir, he may look after himself! A mother, a mother! Ha! ha! *(CAMPBELL laughs. MACKENZIE titters foolishly. CAMPBELL pauses to watch effect of his words.)* Aye, you would think, James, that she would remember the time when he was but little and afraid of all the terrors that walk in darkness, and how he looked up to her as to a tower of safety, and would run to her with outstretched hands, hiding his face from his fear, in her gown. The darkness! It is the dark night and a long journey before him now. *(He pauses again.)* You would think, James, that she would mind how she happit him from the cold of winter and sheltered him from the summer heats, and, when he began to find his footing, how she had an eye on a' the beasts of the field and on the water and the fire that were become her enemies--And to what purpose all this care?--tell me that, my man, to what good, if she is to leave him at the last to dangle from a tree at the end of a hempen rope--to see his flesh given to be meat for the fowls of the air--her son, her little son!

MARY STEWART: My son is guilty of no crime!

CAMPBELL: Is he no'! Weel, mistress, as ye'll no' take my word for it, maybe ye'll list to Mr. Mackenzie here. What say ye, James?

MACKENZIE: He is guilty of aiding and abetting in the concealment of proscribed persons; likewise with being found in the possession of arms, contrary to statute, both very heinous crimes.

CAMPBELL: Very well said, James! Forby, between ourselves, Mrs. Stewart, the young man in my opeenion is guilty of another crime *(snuffs)*--he is guilty of the heinous crime of not knowing on which side his bread is buttered.--Come now--

MARY STEWART: Ye durst not lay a finger on the lad, ye durst not hang him.

MACKENZIE: And why should the gentleman not hang him if it pleesure him?

[CAMPBELL taps snuff-box and takes pinch.]

MARY STEWART: (with intensity) Campbell of Kilmhor, lay but one finger on Dugald Stewart and the weight of Ben Cruachan will be light to the weight that will be laid on your soul. I will lay the curse of the seven rings upon your life: I will call up the fires of Ephron, the blue and the green and the gray fires, for the destruction of your soul: I will curse you in your homestead and in the wife it shelters and in the children that will never bear your name. Yea, and ye shall be cursed.

CAMPBELL: (Startled--betrays agitation--the snuff is spilled from his trembling hand.)Hoot toot, woman! ye're, ye're--(Angrily) Ye auld beldame, to say such things to me! I'll have ye first whippet and syne droont for a witch. Cursed be thae stubborn and supersteetious cattle! (To SANDEMAN) We should have come in here before him and listened in the barn, Sandeman!

SANDEMAN: Ah, listen behind the door you mean! Now I never thought of that!

CAMPBELL: Did ye not! Humph! Well, no doubt there are a good many things in the universe that yet wait for your thought upon them. What would be your objections, now?

SANDEMAN: There are two objections, Kilmhor, that you would understand.

CAMPBELL: Name them.

SANDEMAN: Well, in the first place, we have not wings like crows to fly--and the footsteps on the snow-- Second point--the woman would have told him we were there.

CAMPBELL: Not if I told her I had power to clap her in Inverness jail.

MARY STEWART: (in contempt) Yes, even if ye had told me ye had power to clap me in hell, Mr. Campbell.

CAMPBELL: Lift me that screeching Jezebel oot o' here; Sandeman, we'll mak' a quick finish o' this. (Soldiers take her towards barn.) No, not there; pitch the old girzie into the snow.

MARY STEWART: Ye'll never find him, Campbell, never, never!

CAMPBELL: (enraged) Find him! Aye, by God I'll find him, if I have to keek under every stone on the mountains from the Boar of Badenoch to the Sow of Athole. (Old woman and soldiers go outside.) And now, Captain Sandeman, you an' me must have a word or two. I noted your objection to listening ahint doors and so on. Now, I make a' necessary allowances for youth and the grand and magneeficent ideas commonly held, for a little while, in that period. I had them myself. But, man, gin ye had trod the floor of the Parliament Hoose in Edinburry as long as I did, wi' a pair o' thin hands at the bottom o' toom pockets, ye'd ha'e shed your fine notions, as I did. Noo, fine pernickety noansense will no' do in this business--

SANDEMAN: Sir!

CAMPBELL: Softly, softly, Captain Sandeman, and hear till what I have to say. I have noticed with regret several things in your remarks and bearing which are displeasing to me. I would say just one word in your ear; it is this. These things, Sandeman, are not conducive to advancement in His Majesty's service.

SANDEMAN: Kilmhor, I am a soldier, and if I speak out my mind, you must pardon me if my words are blunt. I do not like this work, but I loathe your methods.

CAMPBELL: Mislike the methods you may, but the work ye must do! Methods are my business. Let me tell you the true position. In ae word it is no more and no less than this. You and me are baith here to carry out the proveesions of the Act for the Pacification of the Highlands. That means the cleaning up of a very big mess, Sandeman, a very big mess. Now, what is your special office in this work? I'll tell ye, man; you and your men are just beesoms in the hands of the law-officers of the Crown. In this district, I order and ye soop! *(He indicates door of barn.)* Now soop, Captain Sandeman.

SANDEMAN: *(in some agitation)* What is your purpose? What are you after? I would give something to see into your mind.

CAMPBELL: Ne'er fash aboot my mind: what has a soldier to do with ony mental operations? It's His Grace's orders that concern you. Oot wi' your man and set him up against the wa'.

SANDEMAN: Kilmhor, it is murder--murder, Kilmhor!

CAMPBELL: Hoots, awa', man, it's a thing o' nae special significance.

SANDEMAN: I must ask you for a warrant.

CAMPBELL: Quick then: Mackenzie will bring it out to you.

[CLERK begins writing. SANDEMAN and soldiers lead STEWART outside, CAMPBELL sits till they are out. CLERK finishes, CAMPBELL signs warrant--and former goes. CAMPBELL is alone, save for MORAG CAMERON, who is sitting huddled up on stool by fire, and is unnoticed by CAMPBELL.]

CAMPBELL: *(as one speaking his thoughts aloud)* I've been beaten for a' that. A strange thing, noo. Beforehand I would ha'e said naething could be easier. And yet--and yet--there it is!... It would have been a grand stroke for me.... Cluny--Keppoch--Lochiel, and maybe ... maybe--Hell! when I think of it! Just a whispered word--a mere pointed finger would ha'e telled a'. But no! their visions, their dreams beat me. "You'll be adding to your experience to-night, Mr. Campbell, and have something to put to the other side of it," says he; aye, and by God I have added something to it, and it is a thing I like but little--that a dream can be stronger than a strong man armed.--Here come I, Archibald Campbell of Kilmhor, invested with authority as law-officer of the Crown, bearing in my hand the power of life and death, fire and the sword, backed up by the visible authority of armed men, and yet I am powerless before the dreams of an old woman and a half-grown lad--soldiers and horses and the gallows and yellow gold are less than the wind blowing in their faces.--It is a strange thing that: it is a thing I do not understand.--It is a thing fit to sicken a man against the notion that there are probabeelities on this earth.--have been beaten for a' that. Aye, the pair o' them have beat me--though it's a matter of seconds till one of them be dead.

MORAG: *(starting into upright position and staring at him; her voice is like an echo to his)* Dead!

CAMPBELL: *(turning hastily)* What is that!

MORAG: Is he dead?

CAMPBELL: *(grimly)* Not yet, but if ye'll look through this window *(he indicates window)*presently, ye'll see him gotten ready for death.

[He begins to collect articles of personal property, hat, etc.]

MORAG: I will tell you.

CAMPBELL: *(astounded)* What!

MORAG: I will tell you all you are seeking to know.

CAMPBELL: *(quietly)* Good God, and to think, to think I was on the very act--in the very act of--tell me--tell me at once.

MORAG: You will promise that he will not be hanged?

CAMPBELL: He will not. I swear it.

MORAG: You will give him back to me?

CAMPBELL: I will give him back unhung.

MORAG: Then *(CAMPBELL comes near)*, in a corrie half-way up the far side of Dearig--God save me!

CAMPBELL: Dished after a'. I've clean dished them! Loard, Loard! once more I can believe in the rationality of Thy world. *(Gathers up again his cloak, hat, etc.)* And to think--to think--I was on the very act of going away like a beaten dog!

MORAG: He is safe from hanging now?

CAMPBELL: *(chuckles and looks out at window before replying, and is at door when he speaks)* Very near it, very near it. Listen!

[He holds up his hand--a volley of musketry is heard. KILMHOR goes out, closing the door behind him. After a short interval of silence the old woman enters and advances a few steps.]

MARY STEWART: Did you hear, Morag Cameron, did you hear?

[The girl is sobbing, her head on her arms.]

MARY STEWART: Och! be quiet now; I would be listening till the last sound of it passes into the great hills and over all the wide world.--It is fitting for you to be crying, a child that cannot understand; but water shall never wet eye of mine for Dugald Stewart. Last night I was but the mother of a lad that herded sheep on the Athole hills: this morn it is I that am the mother of a man who is among the great ones of the earth. All over the land they will be telling of Dugald Stewart. Mothers will teach their children to be men by him. High will his name be with the teller of fine tales.--The great men came, they came in their pride, terrible like the storm they were, and cunning with words of guile were they. Death was with them.... He was but a lad, a young lad, with great length of days before him, and the grandeur of the world. But he put it all from him. "Speak," said they, "speak, and life and great riches will be for yourself." But he said no word at all! Loud was the swelling of their wrath! Let the heart of you rejoice, Morag Cameron, for the snow is red with his blood. There are things greater than death. Let them that are children shed the tears.

[She comes forward and lays her hand on the girl's shoulder.]

MARY STEWART: Let us go and lift him into the house, and not be leaving him lie out there alone.

CURTAIN

Who:

    a. Name:

    b. Age:

    c. Nationality or ethnic group:

    d. Gender:

    e. Aliases, if any:

    f. Name of spouse or sweethearts:

    g. Children, if any:

    h. Divorce, if any:

    i. Parents:

    j. Siblings:

    k. Childhood:

    l. Education:

    m. Employment history:

    n. Social class:

What

    a. What major event is being investigated?

    b. What are the person's daily /weekly activities?

    c. If you were to look at this character's personal belongings, what might you learn about your character?

    d. What happened at the end?

When

    a. In what year or era was the person living?

    b. What time of day was it when the major event happened?

    c. What was going on at the time period when this person lived that might have affected his or her situation?

    d. What clothing considerations can be made for the relevant time period? For example, did a long dress make it hard to run?

Where

    a. City, county, shire, country, etc.:

    b. Type of residence:

    c. Road conditions:

    d. Terrain:

How

    a. How did the character come to be in this situation?

    b. How are the characters related or connected to each other?

    c. How did the character behave in the situation?

Why

    a. Why did the character make the choices he/she did?

    b. Why did the character behave the way he/she did toward others?

Connect the Dots

    a. What do you think would happen the following day (i.e., after the conclusion)?

    b. What is the overall theme of the story?

    c. How will the action of this play affect the audience? (What mood might come over them?)

EXERCISE 2.4: Subtext through Voice Inflection

<u>Directions</u>: Access *YouTube* on the Internet and locate Stan Freberg's 1951 comic routine called "John and Marsha," in which Mr. Freberg uses only two words—John and Marsha—to communicate to the listener a story that actually contains a plot. Then, with your classmates, indicate what plot you think Mr. Freberg intended you to see in this presentation.

URL: <www.youtube.com/watch?v=KkfwmB8jeSU>

EXERCISE 2.5: Practicing Subtext through Voice Inflection

<u>Directions</u>: Working with a partner, choose one of the character sets from the list below (or another of interest to you). Discuss with your partner a scene you could create of the John-and-Marsha type, using just two names (or two words). Practice and then present your routine to the class.

1. Mom and kid

2. Two players from opposing teams

3. Two (or three) school girls at a slumber party

4. Teacher and student

5. Boss and employee

6. Two siblings

EXERCISE 2.6: Assessing Character

Directions: The purpose of this exercise is for you to glean what clues you can about a character by examining the set of the play. Four "sets" appear in the pictures below. Assign two or three students (working alone) to each picture. When you receive your character's "set," study it for clues. What "feel" does the place give you regarding the attributes of the person you are to play? When finished, join with the other person who was assigned the same set and share your thoughts about the character. Does one vision seem more likely, or could both be possible under certain circumstances? Explain your thoughts.

Set A

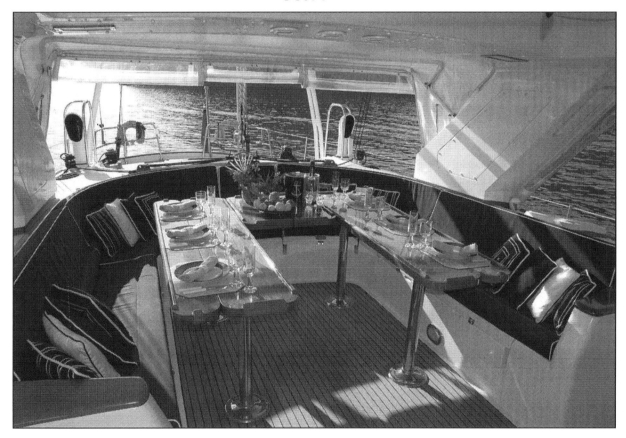

Set B

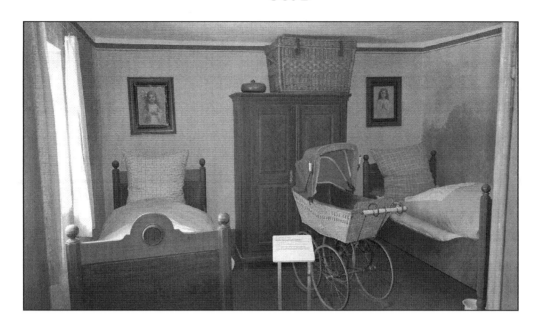

Set C

Set D

Set D

ACTIVITY: Game: "Honey, I love you."

Object of the game: This game is designed to help you practice staying in character.

Method: Arrange the members of the class in a circle. Choose one student to typify the name JOVIAL and send him or her into the circle. JOVIAL approaches another student, who represents SERIOUS, in the circle.

Action:

JOVIAL can use any tone or gesture but may not touch SERIOUS.

JOVIAL begins by saying: "Honey, I love you. Will you please smile for me?"

SERIOUS must maintain eye contact and keep a straight face while responding, "Honey, I love you, but I just can't smile."

Results of Action:

- If JOVIAL makes SERIOUS laugh, SERIOUS must replace JOVIAL in the circle and take the role of JOVIAL.

- If JOVIAL does not succeed in making SERIOUS laugh, JOVIAL moves to another student and repeats the process.

Finish: Play continues until everyone has had an opportunity to play SERIOUS

GREEK THI

Chapter 3

Origins of Theatre in Greece

8th Century BC: The Oral Tradition of Poetry

With the exception of the myth about the goddess Athena springing full-blown from the head of Zeus, nothing really begins fully formed, so the development of theatre in the ancient world must, like everything, be viewed in stages. Theatre has its deepest roots in the earliest period of recorded Greek history, the Archaic Period, which lasted from the eighth to the fifth century BC. The eighth century BC saw the emergence of the great epic poems of Homer, the *Iliad* and the *Odyssey*, which were memorized and recited by a storyteller in what is now called the *oral tradition* of poetry. Most of us know the pleasures of being held spellbound[2] by a good storyteller, say, around the campfire when the night is dark, and the mind is lit by the words of the speaker, the dance of the flames, and the shadows falling across the faces of the listeners. It is an atmosphere that stirs the emotions and enables the imagination to take wing. It must have been so also for the listeners of the single narrator of the oral tradition, who undoubtedly used voice inflections, gesture, and even music like that of the lyre to enhance the experience. Thus was acting born.

7th Century BC: Dithyrambs

The employment of one speaker was also exactly what was used in the presentation of the hymns, or *dithyrambs* [DĬTH-ə-rămz], that were performed by the Greeks at festivals honoring their gods, especially Dionysius [dī-ə-NĬ-əs *or* dī-ə-NĬ-sē- əs], the god of wine and fertility. Originally, the composer of the dithyramb himself would perform the hymn for the audience. Later, a Chorus was added. This was a group of fifty dancers, men and boys, who performed in a circular rotation, probably to the accompaniment of a wind instrument called an *aulos*.

---

[2] The Old English word for *story* was *spell*, which came from the Old Saxon, *spel*, meaning *story*. To be *spellbound*, then, is to be bound strongly by the dramatic power of a story, almost as if bound by the other kind of spell, the witch's spell. The origin and use of this word goes some way toward showing the power of a good storyteller.

From these origins—(a) a single storyteller with the ability to keep a group spellbound and (b) a Chorus of dancers with musical accompaniment—emerged drama.

6th Century BC: Thespis

In the last half of the sixth century BC, a Dionysian priest by the name of Thespis began to take the speaking role, in place of the dithyramb's composer, making him the first actor in the western tradition. To this day, actors and actresses are called thespians in recognition of Thespis' important role in the birth of the theatre.

6th Century BC: The City Dionysia

...arliest dramatic works were written and first ...ned to honor the god Dionysius at the festival in ...called the City Dionysia [dī-ə-NĒ-zhə] Since these ...were held every spring, the playwrights would be ...oughout the rest of the year writing and rehearsing ...plays to present for competition—three tragedies and one satyr play, or farce... ...rd *tragedy* derives from two Greek words—*tragos* ("goat") a... ...—because at the festivals, dancers would sing and dance al... ...uld then be sacrificed to Dionysius. It is also believed that t... ...warded a goat to take home.

5th Century BC: The Grea...

In the fifth century BC—called the Classical period of Greek history—Greek theatre reached its height with the artistry of several great dramatic poets who emerged at that time in Athens, the center of Greek art and culture. These playwrights will be discussed in more detail in the next chapter, but at this point, let us introduce their names:

- Aeschylus [ĔS-kə-ləs], c. 425 – 455 BC

- Sophocles [SŎF-ə-klēz], c. 497 – c. 405 BC

- Euripides [yū-RĬ-pə-dēz], 480 BC – 405 BC

- Aristophanes [ĕ-rĭ-STŎ-fə-nēz], c. 450 – c. 388 BC

Genres

Each type of literature—the play, the poem, the novel, and the short story—is called a *genre* [ZHÄN-rə]. When discussing plays, the genres become more specific: they are classified as either tragedies or comedies.

The classic definition of a tragedy is a play that ends with a death. Indeed, quite often at the end of a Greek tragedy the stage would be strewn with "corpses." Most of the Greek plays which are still taught in schools today are tragedies. *Oedipus Rex, Antigone*, and *Prometheus Bound* still have the power to rouse the emotions.

The classic definition of a comedy is a play that ends with a marriage. The Greek comic plays have been divided into two groups: Old Comedy, which was mainly satire, and New Comedy, which more closely resembles our own definition of comedy. Also ranked as comedy are the *farce*, which included coarse humor, and *satyr plays*, which were definitely not for polite company of refined taste.

Actors

In ancient Greece, only one actor was used in plays until the time of Aeschylus, who introduced the second actor. If multiple charac_ _ were involved, each actor would play more than one part, but the audience _ _nfused because different characters would wear different masks, and it _ _ll an old or young man, an old or young woman, or a boy or gi_ was worn.

How did audience members tell char apart? - mask

Thespis, the first actor, is known to have _ _ e in a wagon in which he carried costumes and masks. Today _ _sses are far more famous than those who compose the plays and movies, _ _ncient theatre, the actors were more likely to be unknown persons of low so_ _ status. And, unlike today's actors and actresses, the players in antiquity were amateurs who worked part-time without pay.

Throughout the classical period and through the sixteenth century, all parts were played by men or boys.

Soc (470-399)
Plato (437-347)
Arist (384-222)

Structure of the Theatre

Theatre of Dionysius at Athens, 2nd century AD

The first stone theatre in Greece was the Theatre of Dionysius in Athens, which was built on the south slope of the Acropolis, probably in the late sixth century. The stone theatre still visited by tourists to Athens dates from the second century AD. The original theatre has long since disappeared except for some of the foundations, which are still visible. The Greek theatre established an architectural pattern which, with some modifications as technology became more advanced, still defines theatres today. The parts of the Greek theatre are explained below.

Orchestra

In English, the word *orchestra* refers to players of music, but the original term meant "dancing place." It was the circular (later, semi-circular) area where both the dialogue of the actors and the singing and dancing of the Chorus were presented. Originally unpaved, it graduated to marble as the city grew in wealth and prestige.

Altar

In the center of the orchestra was an altar, called a *thymele* [THĬM-ə-lā], which signified the religious nature of the dramatic festivals. At the City Dionysius, it would be used for the sacrifice of a goat or, according to Plato, a pig.

Theatron (Koilon, Cavea)

Our word *theatre* derives from the Greek word *theatron* [thē-Ä-trən], which was the "seeing place," the area where the spectators sat. Textbooks often refer to this area with the Latin word *cavea*, which was the equivalent of the Greek word *koilon*, or "hollow," so called because the earliest theatres were built in the hollows of mountains. In that way, the slope of the mountain could support the theatre's rising rows of seats.

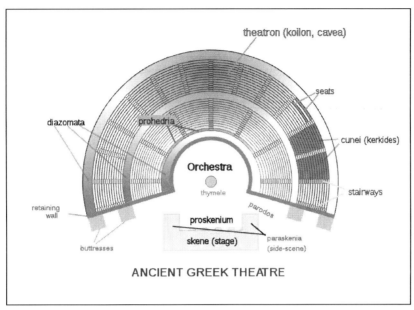

Figure 2: Parts of the Greek theatre

As in sports stadiums today, the cavea was divided into wedge-shaped sections (the *cunei*) separated by aisles for the use of the spectators. The grassy area that separated the orchestra from the audience was called the *prohedria*, the same term being used to refer to the first few rows of seating, which were reserved for the important people of the city. People could move from one side of the theatre to the other by using the semicircular passages called the *diazomata*.

Skene

Our word *scene* derives from the Greek word *skene* [SKĀ-nə], which meant *tent*. In the theatre, the skene was a small wooden structure used to store costumes and masks and served as a changing place for the actors as well. Since these small buildings were typically made of wood, the earliest skenes have not survived, though the foundations are often still visible.

Proskenion

The Greek stage had no curtains, but today the terms *proscenium* [prō-SĒ-nē-əm] and *proscenium arch* refer to the area of the stage in front of the curtain. This word derives from the Greek word *proskenion* [prō-SKĀ-nē-ŏn], which consists of the prefix *pro-* ("in front of") added to the root word *skene*—the area in front of the skene.

Paraskenia

The word *paraskenia* [pæ-rə-SKĀ-nē-ə] consists of the prefix *para-* ("beside") added to the root word *skene* and refers to the two wings on either side of the skene. This was an area where special effects technicians could work, shaking pebbles in bronze containers to simulate the sound of thunder, for example.

Parados

The word *parados* [PÆ-rə-dŏs] ("byway") refers to the passageway through which spectators entered the *theatron* and actors entered the stage.

Size of the Theatre

By 330 BC, the theatre at Athens had grown so large it could hold 17,000 people. It is fairly obvious that people sitting in the top row would not have been able to see the actors or the masks well, but, as explained below, we now know they were able to hear as clearly as those on the first row.

The size of the stage itself would have been considerably smaller than that of today's theatre. One scholar has calculated that, allowing a 70′ diameter for an orchestra (the one at Athens was only 66′), the depth of the Greek stage would have been approximately 10′ or less.[12] This is two feet shorter than the length of an average living room [typically 12′ x 12′] in a small home in the United States. However, perhaps this was enough even when three actors became the norm in the plays of Sophocles.

Acoustics

Writing in the first century BC, the Roman architect Vitruvius commented on the methods of the Greek architects, saying: "By the rules of mathematics and the method of music, they sought to make the voices from the stage rise more clearly and sweetly to the spectators' ears." He explained that their technology also involved bronze vessels full of water which were placed in niches under the seats.[13]

The scientific principles of sound that Vitruvius mentioned are known as *acoustics* [ə-KŪ-stĭks], which derives from the Greek word *akouein*, "to hear." Knowledge of the acoustics of a Greek theatre was greatly enhanced in 1881 when the Greek archaeologist Panagís Kavadías discovered and began unearthing the long-buried theatre at Epidaurus. This theatre was designed by the Greek architect Polykleitos the Younger around 340-350 BC and was built into the west side of Mount Kynortio, which has a slope of 26°. In 2007, a team from the Georgia Institute of Technology, led by Nico Declercq and Cindy Dekeyser, set out to solve the mystery of the theatre's acoustics. They eventually figured out that the limestone steps, moving upward from the orchestra to the highest row of seats, acted as "acoustic traps." These steps prevented low-frequency sound, such as wind and the scuffling of spectators, from rising, but passed on high-frequency sound, such as the voices of the actors.[14] Knowing this, it is hard to understand why such theatres did not make the list of the wonders of the ancient world.

ACTIVITY: Building a Theatre

Directions: The purpose of this activity is to familiarize you with the construction and parts of a Greek theatre. Work in groups of three to five members to construct a theatre model, following the specifications below.

Materials: You may use any materials, such as Legos, sugar cubes, candies, Popsicle sticks, cardboard, or other craft materials (preferably something you already have on hand).

Specifications:

- Make a 3-dimensional model (not a drawing).

- Label all the parts of the theatre. Refer to the terms and diagrams in this chapter for assistance with this.

- Allow a base of about 12 inches to 18 inches.

- Make sure each student has a role in creating the model.

Presentation:

- Every student must have a part in the presentation.

- The group needs to point out all the parts of the theatre.

- Prepare as if you were giving this presentation to Kindergartners. How would you make it interesting for them?

- The presentation needs to be rehearsed.

- It needs to keep the attention of the class. Employ good eye contact with the audience, good projection, and good voice inflection.

Objections to the Theatre in Ancient Greece

Writing in the late seventh century BC or early sixth century BC, the prophet Jeremiah recorded the words of the Lord to his people, concerning the false (or "lying") prophets among them: "Do not listen to the words of the prophets who prophesy to you, filling you with vain hopes. They speak visions of their own minds, not from the mouth of the LORD." This and other passages of Scripture help to explain the longstanding Judeo-Christian objection to the theatre—the fear of the corruption of the mind by those who spread the thoughts not of the Lord, but of their own minds in their plays. Quite possibly, you have heard something similar from your own parents, who may closely check a movie's rating before granting permission for you to watch. The tendency is for teenagers to consider their parents "old fogeys" when it comes to decisions of this sort, but the objections of Christian parents are by no means the first to be leveled at the "visions" of a playwright or screenwriter. Such objections reach all the way back to the Golden Age of Athens when Plato launched an invective against the theatre so vivid that Aristotle later thought it necessary to put things into perspective by setting standards for the artistic uses of the theatre. Their thoughts appear below.

Plato

Plato (c. 428-347 BC) wrote much in the *Republic* about the city being the guardians of the people, and, in this context, he actually advocated censorship in order to protect the minds of the citizens. His first reference to censorship concerns the education of children. In this text, which is in the form of a conversation, the main speaker is Socrates, who asks questions in the form of what we now call *Socratic dialogue.*

And shall we just carelessly allow children to hear any casual tales which may be devised by casual persons, and to receive into their minds ideas for the most part the very opposite of those which we should wish them to have when they are grown up?

We cannot.

Then the first thing will be to establish a censorship of the writers of fiction, and let the censors receive any tale of fiction which is good, and reject the bad; and we will desire mothers and nurses to tell their children the authorised ones only. Let them fashion the mind with such tales, even more fondly than they mould the body with their hands; but most of those which are now in use must be discarded.[15]

Greek plays often told of the activities of the gods and goddesses. Imagine having deities so evil that their doings needed to be banned from the ears of the young, but this is exactly what Plato advised:

The doings of Cronus, and the sufferings which in turn his son inflicted upon him, even if they were true, ought certainly not to be lightly told to young and thoughtless persons; if possible, they had better be buried in silence. But if there is an absolute necessity for their mention, a chosen few might hear them in a mystery, and they should sacrifice not a common pig, but some huge and unprocurable victim; and then the number of the hearers will be very few indeed. . . .

Neither, if we mean our future guardians to regard the habit of quarrelling among themselves as of all things the basest, should any word be said to them of the wars in heaven, and of the plots and fightings of the gods against one another, for they are not true. No, we shall never mention the battles of the giants, or let them be embroidered on garments; and we shall be silent about the innumerable other quarrels of gods and heroes with their friends and relatives. If they would only believe us we would tell them that quarrelling is unholy, and that never up to this time has there been any quarrel between citizens; this is what old men and old women should begin by telling children; and when they grow up the poets also should be told to compose for them in a similar spirit. But the narrative of Hephaestus binding Hera, his mother, or how on another occasion Zeus sent him flying for taking her part when she was being beaten, and all the battles of the gods in Homer—these tales must not be admitted into our State, whether they are supposed to have an allegorical meaning or not. For a young person cannot judge what is allegorical and what is literal; anything that he receives into his mind at that age is likely to become indelible and unalterable; and therefore it is most important that the tales which the young first hear should be models of virtuous thoughts.[16]

But Plato did not address his concerns about the young only. He goes on to say that poets manipulated the emotions of all theatergoers. As he put it, "The imitative poet (playwright) implants an evil constitution, for he indulges the irrational nature" of humankind. Thus, plays had "the power of harming even the good."[17] These comments illustrate how, even in the earliest stages of drama, wise people were expressing great concerns about the potentially negative impact of the theatre on human behavior.

Aristotle

Aristotle (d. 322 BC) was the student of Plato, and some scholars believe that when Aristotle wrote the *Poetics*, he was making a rebuttal of what Plato had said. Certainly he did not call for censorship or object to stories about the quarrels of the gods. However, he did show that he understood Plato's concern, objecting specifically to playwrights "who are censured for representing degraded women."[18] In addition, he gave playwrights four principles to follow when developing character: "Now any speech or action that manifests moral purpose of any kind will be expressive of character: the character will be good if the purpose is good."[19]

By insisting that the character of the hero be good, he implies that the opposite would also be true. In other words, the presentation of an evil hero would be immoral. Aristotle lived in a culture far different from our own and had not been introduced to the idea that all people are equal in the sight of God. The position of women and of slaves was very low in Greek culture, but Aristotle did offer this as a guideline for the playwrights who introduced female and slave characters: "This rule [about the goodness of the characters] is relative to each class. Even a woman may be good, and also a slave; though the woman may be said to be an inferior being, and the slave quite worthless."[20] Though this is shocking to us, the most important thing to notice here is that Aristotle reminded playwrights that women and slaves need not be represented as evil on the stage.

So, along with the origin of the theatre came the origin of criticism of the theatre, including moral and ethical objections. As theatre took a dark turn in the Roman period, the criticism of the theatre was also ramped up, as we shall see in Chapter 7.

ARISTOTLE'S *POETICS*

Chapter 4

Introduction

The work which established the standards for the literature of western civilization was the *Poetics* of Aristotle, which was composed in 350 BC. After briefly discussing comedy, this work laid out the basic elements and principles of tragedy, elements which still separate quality literature from those works called "pulp fiction," escapist novels, or B-movies. The purpose of this chapter is to introduce Aristotle's principles and give you the opportunity to see them at work in various plays.

Aristotle (384-322 BC)

Aristotle's Insights on Origins

According to Aristotle, great epic poems like the *Iliad* and the *Odyssey* developed gradually into the type of literature called tragedy, which became a staple of Greek drama.

> As, in the serious style, Homer is pre-eminent among poets, for he alone combined dramatic form with excellence of imitation so he too first laid down the main lines of comedy, by dramatizing the ludicrous instead of writing personal satire. His *Margites* bears the same relation to comedy that the *Iliad* and *Odyssey* do to tragedy. But when Tragedy and Comedy came to light, the two classes of poets still followed their natural bent: the lampooners became writers of Comedy, and the Epic poets were succeeded by Tragedians, since the drama was a larger and higher form of art.[21]

Aristotle's Theory of Tragedy

Though Aristotle briefly discussed comedy in the *Poetics*, he preferred tragedy as the best way to examine the human condition. He defined tragedy as the imitation of an action that is (a) serious, (b) complete (having a beginning, a middle, and end), (c) written in pleasurable language, (d) presented in dramatic rather than narrative (or story) form, and (e) centered on incidents that will arouse the emotions of pity and fear.

Tragedy was to represent not just a series of actions, but a change of fortune from happiness to misery. It was intended to evoke feelings of fear and pity in the audience—the same kind of fear and pity that is represented in the saying, "There but for the grace of God, go I," the statement of Englishman John Bradford (1510-1555) upon seeing a group of men being led to their execution. In such cases, one often thinks, "How terrible if that would happen to me! What can I do to prevent it?"

Six Principles

In the *Poetics*, Aristotle explained the six principles of a dramatic work and established some rules (or "best practices"). He arranged them in order of importance with the most important (Action) being first and the least important (Spectacle) being last.

Action (Plot)

Aristotle divided a play into three parts, which he named simply the Beginning, the Middle, and the End. It is tempting to think of these three parts as three acts, though Aristotle did not use that term.

The problem in the play was often caused by events that preceded the **Beginning** of the play. For example, in Aeschylus' play *The Persians*, the army of Xerxes had been defeated by the Greeks in the Battle of Salamis before the beginning of the play. That defeat triggered the action of the play. According to Aristotle, the action of the play was a chain of causes and effects (termed *complications*) that led inevitably to a certain outcome. That is to say, A would lead to B, B would lead to C, and so on to the end.

This chain of causes and effects created rising action toward the **Middle** of the play, which is typically called the *climax* of the play. Due perhaps to the influence of

Hollywood, the term *dramatic climax*, as it is used today, often refers to an exciting finish that resolves a problem. However, the classic term referred to that point in the play where the condition of the hero changes from fortunate to unfortunate. From that change in fortune, the play goes into *falling action*, in which the suffering of the hero takes place (e.g., defeat, suicide, mutilation, murder, exile).

And finally a play reaches its **End**, which is called the *catastrophe*—"how things turn out," so to speak. The original Greek word *catastrophe* was the equivalent of the English word *overturning*. The idea was that the fortunes of the protagonist had been completely overturned from happiness to loss. However, because of the strong influence of Greek tragedy, where the catastrophe involved such things as defeat, murder, or suicide, the word *catastrophe*, as it is now used in English, refers only to bad outcomes. To understand Aristotle's use of the word, one can point out Aristotle's statement that in plays which have two threads (one involving evil and one, good) there might be different catastrophes (one bad, one good).[22]

We might imagine these three parts of a play in the form of a triangle, thus:

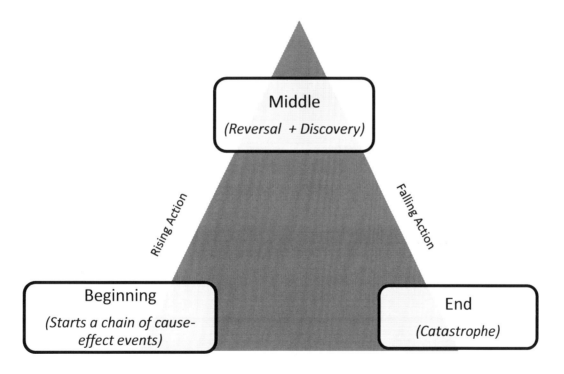

Plot Structure as explained by Aristotle, 350 BC

Some of the rules that govern plot structure, according to Aristotle, were these:

- The play should not simply be a string of episodes which have no overall connection to one another. Rather, the plot must involve a change of fortune for the hero—from good to bad.

- The plot should contain three parts:

    o First, *peripeteia* [pār-ĭ-pə-TĒ-ə], a sudden reversal in fortune

    o Second, *anagnorisis* [ăn-ĭg-NŌ-rĭ-sĭs], the moment of discovery when the hero becomes aware of his misfortune

    o Third, *pathos* [PĀ-thōs], a scene of suffering

- Except in cases involving Fate, such as that expressed by an oracle at Delphi, the plot should not depend on coincidence or the random appearance of a god.

- The plot should contain only the chain of necessary causes and effects that change the fortune of the hero. (No extraneous material should be included.)

Character

Aristotle set forth in his *Poetics* what he considered to be the best character for a Tragedy—the *tragic hero*. The tragic hero is the character who undergoes a change of fortune from happiness to misery. But his or her downfall is brought about not as the result of a sin or an evil nature, but as a result of some error in judgment or character flaw, which is termed the *tragic flaw*. The tragic flaw is that character trait which

Ajax as depicted by J. C. Andrä, 1902

normally would be considered a strength, but which turns out to be the cause of the character's change from happiness to misery. One character who typifies the tragic hero and the tragic flaw is Ajax, whose desire to be the best Greek warrior got the best of him when someone else was awarded the armor of Achilles. At that point, he was overcome with such jealousy that he went on a rampage and ended by killing himself.

In the *Poetics*, Aristotle set out standards for the tragic hero, which have been followed, for the most part, ever since.

- First, not just anyone could be the hero of a tragic play. Aristotle argued that the best tragedies were those which concerned the misfortunes "of a few houses," or great families, by which he meant the great royal families of Greek mythology—those "who have done or suffered something terrible."[23] Sophocles' plays about King Oedipus are good examples.

- Second, the tragic figure is to be a person of good character and moral purpose.

- Third, playwrights should aim at propriety in drawing their characters. A man of his times, Aristotle illustrated his point by saying that it would be inappropriate for a woman to show manly valor. He also thought that though cleverness might be a good quality, "unscrupulous cleverness" would be inappropriate since such a character would no longer typify good character.

- Fourth, the tragic character is to be realistic.

- Last, the personality of the tragic figure is to be consistent. For example, it would not make sense for a character to be shy in one scene and flirtatious in another. However, if inconsistency is actually to be the main trait of the character, then the character should be "consistently inconsistent."

Thought

Important to Aristotle's concept of tragedy is the idea that the play was to offer the audience some insight into human behavior. That is to say, more than just entertaining folks for ninety minutes, a play should cause a person to think. For this reason, Aristotle listed Thought as the third element of tragedy. He explained the element by defining it as the articulation of a general truth, a maxim. For an example, we can look at Aeschylus' play *The Persians,* in which the ghost of Darius states the maxim, "Treasured riches naught avail the dead."[24]

In discovering the idea of a play or novel, today's reader has the advantage of the work of Mortimer Adler (1902-2001), who identified what he called "the 103 Great Ideas" of Western literature. One of the Ideas he listed is Wealth, which certainly applies to the maxim of Darius quoted above. Other examples are Good and Evil, Life and Death, Fate, Religion, and Tyranny. Such ideas were certainly explored in the great Greek tragedies. The writer's idea about such a matter was (and still is) the playgoer's main "take-away" from a play, a source of lasting pleasure to consider, compare, and debate with others.

Diction

Diction refers to the artistic use of language. As indicated above, Aristotle believed that a good play was to have "pleasurable language," and he provided several examples of what a good writer can do with words.

- First, a writer can coin new words. For example, in *Prometheus Bound*, Aeschylus created the word *starry-kirtled* (ποικιλείμων) to describe the night.

- Second, a writer can use words as metaphors (comparisons). In *Antigone*, for example, Sophocles called the sun the "eye of golden day."

- Third, a word can be ornamental, said Aristotle, by which he meant that words can be highly descriptive. Some especially descriptive phrases can be found in Aeschylus' play *Ajax,* where we read how Ajax "raved in maniac throes" and with his "reeking sword" went "plunging amid the thronging horns" of animals, committing mass slaughter on "herds and flocks, their guardians dead beside them."

- Some of Aristotle's examples of word play were based on the unique characteristics of the Greek language, but some of them are applicable to English. For example, he pointed out that words can be contracted for special effect. The Scottish poet Charles Gray (1782-1851) gives several examples of this in his poem "Epistle to ALJ," where these three lines appear:

> Yet had he looket sharp around
> Enow o' trees he might hae found
> To hang a' rogues on English ground.[25]

In three lines, Gray used four contractions: (a) the word *enough* appears as *enow*, (b) *of* appears as *o'*, (c) *have* appears as *hae* (which is typical of the Scots dialect), and (d) *all* appears as *a'*. Thus, contraction has served as a main feature of Gray's diction.

- Writers sometimes employ what Aristotle called "strange" or foreign words. In English-language literature, too, one sometimes finds words drawn from earlier periods of the language, as in J. R. R. Tolkein's *Lord of the Rings* trilogy, which frequently used words from Old English, the form of English spoken from about AD 500 to 1100. For example, he gave Saruman's fortress the name *Isengard*, which derives from the Old English words *isen* (meaning *iron*) and *gard* (meaning *enclosure*).[26]

In addition to these principles, one cannot neglect the numerous figures of speech (tropes) that work to create rich diction. As can be seen in the list that follows, these tropes usually have Greek names that reveal their origin among the Greek poets. Here are a few examples from Greek tragedies:

- **Simile:** A comparison using *like* or *as*. Sophocles used a simile in his play *Electra*, when Orestes, who has returned home to avenge his father's murder, says: "I trust from this rumor I also shall emerge in radiant life, and yet *shine like a star* upon my foes."

- **Alliteration:** The repetition of the same sound at the beginning of adjacent (or nearly adjacent) words. For example, as Electra encourages her brother Orestes to take vengeance on Aegisthus, she says, "Slay him forthwith, and *cast* his *corpse* to the *creatures* from whom such as he should have burial, far from our sight!"

- **Periphrasis:** Circumlocution, a longer and wordier manner of speech than is necessary. Aeschylus was particularly fond of this technique. Though used nowadays primarily for comic effect, in the Greek plays it was often tied to the use of an oracle or riddle—two indirect ways of stating something simple. One well-known example is the riddle of the Sphinx, which King

Oedipus pondering the riddle of the Sphinx.

Oedipus was finally able to solve. The riddle asked, "What walks on four feet in the morning, two in the afternoon, and three at night?" Oedipus answered: "Man: as an infant, he crawls on all fours; as an adult, he walks on two legs and; in old age, he uses a 'walking' stick." In this example, we would say that "an animal that walks on four feet in the morning, two in the afternoon, and three at night" is a circumlocution for the word *man*. It is said that Aeschylus included this riddle in his satyr play, *The Sphinx*, though the text has not survived.

- **Accumulation:** A heaping up of metaphors or descriptions beyond what is necessary to make the simple point. In Aeschylus' play *Agamemnon*, for example, the Greeks have returned from the Trojan War, and the leader of the Chorus launches into a monologue describing all the woes the men experienced in their battles. As seen by the bold-faced phrases in the excerpt below, he even moves the speech along with questions to the effect, "Why tell this? Why go into that?" And yet he does, on and on, thus:

> **I could a tale unfold of toiling oars**,
> Ill rest, scant landings on a shore rock-strewn,
> All pains, all sorrows, for our daily doom.
> **And worse and hatefuller our woes on land;**
> For where we couched, close by the foeman's wall,
> The river-plain was ever dank with dews,
> Dropped from the sky, exuded from the earth,
> A curse that clung unto our sodden garb,
> And hair as horrent as a wild beast's fell.
> **Why tell the woes of winter**, when the birds
> Lay stark and stiff, so stern was Ida's snow?
> **Or summer's scorch**, what time the stirless wave
> Sank to its sleep beneath the noon-day sun?
> **Why mourn old woes?** Their pain has passed away;
> And passed away, from those who fell, all care,
> For evermore, to rise and live again.
> **Why sum the count of death**, and render thanks
> For life by moaning over fate malign?
> Farewell, a long farewell to all our woes![27]

These and many more figures of speech (tropes) are used in a great work of literature to create the author's style and elevate the diction in the work.

Song

When Aristotle referred to the element of Song in Greek tragedies, he was referring to the Greek Chorus. Aristotle considered the Chorus to be an actor on the stage. Its purpose was to comment on the action of the play, serve as narrator to move the plot along, and to heighten the mood of the piece.

He advocated for the Chorus to be considered an actor and to be an "integral" part of the play's action.[28] By that, he meant that if the Chorus were removed from the play, it would not make sense; it would fall apart.

What exactly was the Greek Chorus?

Six members of the Chorus listen to a speech by King Oedipus in a Spanish production of *Edipo Rei (Oedipus Rex)*, 2011. CC By 2.0.

The Greek Chorus was a group of singers, or chanters, composed originally of fifty members, but whittled down to twelve in the later period. They were all males, and, as a matter of fact, were typically students studying music at the schools. Now, this does not simply mean that there were students who trained their voices in a music class, as we might think of school music today. Greek education consisted of the *trivium* (grammar, logic, and rhetoric) as well as the *quadrivium* (the four aspects of mathematics: arithmetic, geometry, music, and astronomy). Since music was taught as a form of mathematics, we can conclude that it was not simply a form of entertainment. As seen in Chapter 3, the great playwright Sophocles is known to have led the Chorus in Athens' celebration of the Greek victory at the Battle of Salamis when he was only fifteen. The thought that he formed a part of the Chorus in other Greek plays current in his day is supported by the phrase "You, Sophocles, who sang with choruses," which was discovered in the *Palatine Anthology*.[29]

The Chorus performed in the area of the Greek stage called the orchestra, but it would be a mistake to think of the Chorus and the orchestra in the same way we think of it today. A Greek Chorus did not actually sing. Rather, they spoke, or chanted, in unison. Nor was their much in the way of musical instruments, if any. What exactly did they chant, and how could chanting be called "melodic"?

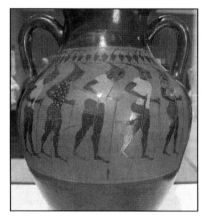

Pottery image of a Chorus of stilt-walkers

The Greek Chorus chanted poetry in the form of odes (Greek *ōidē*), which were lyrical (i.e., emotional) stanzas originally created to offer praises to a god. The play would open with an ode (called a *parados*) and close with an ode (called an *exodus*). An ode was divided into three parts, each involving a specific movement on the stage. In the first part, called the *strophe* [STRŌ-fē], the Chorus would move to the left. In the second part, called the *antistrophe* [ăn-TĬ-strō-fē], the Chorus moved back to the right. Sometimes a final stanza called an *epode* [Ĕ-pōd] was included, in which the Chorus moved to the center of the stage.

Authorities differ as to whether or not the Chorus was accompanied by instruments. The words were always much more important to the Greeks than the sounds of the instruments. The role of the poet was to create beauty through language alone. This idea is not totally unfamiliar to students of the Bible, since the arrangement and melody of the Greek odes was equally valued by the Old Testament psalmists. As William Willis Moseley once wrote, the Greek odes were "like the sacred songs of Moses, David, and Isaiah without rhyme or metre; whose odes had a syllabic quantity only."[30] Moseley added a note from the writings of Dr. Hugh Blair, who observed, "They rested the melody of their verse on the number of their syllables."[31]

In summary, the Greek Chorus was a group from twelve to fifty male "singers," who chanted odes that moved the action along and commented on the events of the play.

EXERCISE 3.1: Practicing Strophe and Antistrophe

Directions: In 1902, Richard G. Moulton, professor of English literature at the University of Chicago, published a work entitled *Select Masterpieces of Biblical Literature* and sub-titled *The Modern Reader's Bible: A Series of Works from the Sacred Scriptures Presented in Modern Literary Form*.   Included in the work was "Deborah's Song" from the fifth chapter of Judges.   In the excerpt printed below, please notice how Moulton applied the strophe and antistrophe of the Greek chorus to Judges 5:19-23, assigning the strophes to the men and the antistrophes to the women.   With your classmates, present this passage, moving from right to left with the strophe and left to right with the antistrophe.   If time permits, have the young men in the class memorize the strophes and the young women, the antistrophes.

INTRODUCTION: "Deborah's Song" is a victory hymn about the Israelites' defeat of the Canaanites, which was sung by Deborah and Barak.

Excerpt from Deborah's Song (Judges 5:19-23)
Part 3: The Battle and the Rout

Strophe
Men.
The kings came and fought;
    Then fought the kings of Canaan,
In Taanach by the waters of Megiddo:—
    They took no gain of money!

Antistrophe
Women.
They fought from heaven,
    The stars in their courses fought against Sisera.
The river Kishon swept them away,—
    That ancient river, the river Kishon!

O, my soul, march on with strength!

Strophe

Men.

O my soul, march on with strength!

 Then did the horsehoofs stamp

By reason of the pransings,[3]

 The pransings of their strong ones.

Antistrophe

Women.

Curse ye Meroz, said the angel of the LORD,

 Curse ye bitterly the inhabitants thereof;

Because they came not to the help of the LORD,

 To the help of the LORD against the mighty![32]

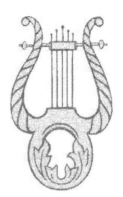

Spectacle

The last of Aristotle's six components of tragedy was Spectacle, which he considered the least important of the components. Nowadays, we might refer to this aspect of the theatre as "special effects," and our emphasis on technical wizardry today has elevated the importance of spectacle in stagecraft. However, the Greeks thought differently. They placed much more emphasis on the language of the play—the speeches and the emotional displays of the actors. Aristotle was almost snobbish about Spectacle, saying that "the production of spectacular effects depends more on the art of the stage machinist than that of the poet." In short, he believed that Spectacle was the "least artistic" element of a play and "connected least with the art of poetry."[33]

This idea sounds strange to those of us who have become accustomed to both computer-generated effects in movies and special machinery for the stage. Theatre-goers were perhaps not totally astounded by the stage installed in London's Drury Lane Theatre in 2007 for a performance of J. R. R. Tolkien's *Lord of the Rings*. Not only was the stage operated by seventeen pneumatic lifts boasting three revolving turntables, but the three turntables could also be raised and lowered independently of each other. Such elaborate contraptions are not without their dangers, however. In

---

[3] According to Strong's Concordance, *pransing* (or, as some might spell it, *prancing*) is the seventeenth-century English translation of the Hebrew word *daharah* (galloping).

May 2007, at a preview performance of the play, somehow an actor's leg was suddenly caught in the rotating stage, and the performance was forced to a halt.

Of course, folks living in the sixth century BC did not have the highly developed equipment that we have now, but they were certainly busy creating it. Once Greek architects had invented a crane to raise blocks of stone in construction work, the theatre directors were quick to see how they could use such a device to enhance the dramatic experience for theatregoers. Certainly some scripts reveal that actors representing gods and goddesses were delivering their lines as they were being lowered onto the stage "from the heavens," so to speak. One example appears in the play *Prometheus Bound*, in which Zeus has bound Prometheus on a mountaintop as punishment for giving humans the gift of fire. While there, he is visited by characters arriving by air, as these lines spoken by the Chorus reveal:

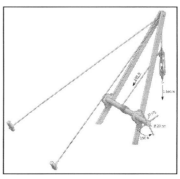

A Greco-Roman trispastos (3-pulley-crane) able to lift about 330 pounds.

> Prometheus, we have heard thy call:
> Not on deaf ears these awful accents fall.
> Lo! lightly leaving at thy words
> *My flying car*
> *And holy air*, the pathway of great birds,
> I long to tread this land of peak and scar. . . .[34] [emphasis added]

Deus ex machina

This theatrical device is called by the Latin phrase *deus ex machina* [DĀ-əs ĕks MĂK-ĭ-nə], or "god from the machine." (Aristotle, who coined the term, used the Greek equivalent, of course: *apò mēkhanês theós*.) The crane would be placed on top of the skene, and by means of ropes, pulleys, and a sizable basket, an actor could make his entrance from above the stage rather than from the *parados* on the side of the stage where, of course, mere mortals continued to enter and exit. All things considered, it might be reasonable to speculate that an actor in ancient Greece, not unlike the poor fellow in London in 2007, might also have been injured in a mishap with the machine.

It is important also to note that the term *deus ex machina* refers not only to the machine itself, but to a plot trick that Aristotle discouraged in the construction of a play. Aristotle insisted that plot be based on what was probable, a logical sequence of causes and effects. He wrote that "the unraveling of the plot . . . must arise out of the plot itself, it must not be brought about by the *deus ex machina*,"[35] and he disapproved of the tale of Medea where, after the murder of her children, Medea is allowed to escape her well-deserved punishment by being drawn upward in her serpent-drawn chariot, a gift from the god Helios. Aristotle believed such gimmicks left the audience unsatisfied and thought they would much prefer to know that Medea had gotten what was coming to her.

A better use of the *deus ex machina* is in *Prometheus Bound*, where the god Oceanus descends from the heavens to the mountaintop to offer Prometheus advice about how to handle Zeus. Since the Greeks considered it natural for the gods to take on this kind of role, a visitor from heaven would have been quite logical to them. It might, in fact, be seen as more probable than a human being climbing all the way to the top of a mountain for a friendly little chat. When finished with his conversation, Oceanus flies back heavenward. He has not interfered with the punishment Zeus inflicted, and the audience still has the satisfaction of seeing how things will turn out.[36]

In addition to the *deus ex machina*, the Greeks invented a platform on wheels in order to create what is called a *tableau* [tăb-LŌ]. The tableau is familiar to us today in the "living nativity scenes" presented by some churches at Christmastime—not a dramatization of the Christmas story, but just a scene with costumed people and perhaps a manger animal or two.

But how could a silent tableau be used in a play where speaking was paramount? It was exactly because the Greeks valued the language of the play more than the "action" on the stage that violent acts—such as combat, murder, and suicide—occurred off-stage and were simply narrated onstage by a messenger who arrived with the news. Still, in their desire to enhance the "fear and pity" to be aroused in the audience, the Greeks designed a wheeled platform which could be rolled out of a door in the skene in order to exhibit, say, the bodies of the slain. This device was called an *eccyclema* [ĕk-zĭ-KLĒ-mə] (based on the words *ek*, "out of," and *kyklein*, "to wheel"). At the end of *Agamemnon,* for example, the corpses of Agamemnon and Cassandra were rolled out on the eccyclema by an actor in the role of a family servant, followed by Clytemenestra still wielding her axe. Aristotle may have had such tableaux in mind when he wrote that poets should construct their plays so that "even without the aid of the eye, he who hears the tale told will thrill with horror and melt to pity at what takes place. . . . But to produce this effect by the mere spectacle is a less artistic method. . . . Those who employ spectacular means to create a sense not of the terrible but only of the monstrous, are strangers to the purpose of Tragedy."[37]

Entry through which the *eccyclema* could be wheeled in the Roman theatre at Bosra, Syria

Summing up, the six elements of tragedy laid out in order of importance by Aristotle are Action, Character, Thought, Diction, Song, and Spectacle.

Aristotle's Comments on Comedy

Aristotle had much less to say about comedy than tragedy, but he did have some key ideas.

First, like tragedy, a comedy should imitate real-life behavior. However, whereas tragedy may be about gods and kings (those who are "better" than the average person), comedy is about those who are "worse" than the average person. Therefore, though comic figures may undergo a change in fortune from good to bad, they do not inspire pity. Instead, they simply become objects of ridicule.

Aristotle stated that comedy had its origins in Megara, a town in western Attica, where a poet named Epicharmus would even write comedies that poked fun at the gods: "The gods are winds, water, earth, sun, fire, stars. But I've come to the conclusion that for us the only useful gods are silver and gold."[38]

Now, humor like this that pokes fun at gods and human rulers is called *satire*, whereas humor that is designed simply to be silly is called *farce*. Greek comedies consisted mainly of satire, which was often full of harsh invective, as in *The Frogs* by Aristophanes where the poets Euripides and Aeschylus go at each other in this way:

EURIPIDES (*of Aeschylus*)
I know the man, I've scanned him through and through,
A savage-creating stubborn-pulling fellow,
Uncurbed, unfettered, uncontrolled of speech,
Unperiphrastic, bombastiloquent.

AESCHYLUS
Hah! sayest thou so, child of the garden quean,
And this to me, thou chattery-babble-collector,
Thou pauper-creating rags-and-patches-stitcher?
Thou shale abye° it dearly![39]   °pay the penalty for

A satyr-like Satan baptizes a disciple.

The other kind of humor, *farce*, is found in what was called the *satyr play*, which is named after the satyr of Greek mythology, a figure that was half-man and half-goat and knew no moral bounds. In the Old Testament, the word *satyr* is clearly associated with evil and ruin, as shown in the passage about God's destruction of Babylon, where we read: "But wild beasts of the desert shall lie there; and their houses shall be full of doleful creatures; and owls shall dwell there, and satyrs shall dance there" (Is. 13:21, KJV). Over the centuries, Christian art has frequently pictured Satan as a satyr, as in the image above from the sixteenth century.

In twenty-first century terms, we might say the satyr plays were R-rated comedies where characters employed what English-speakers call "four-letter words" to get a laugh. Aristotle disdained this type of play and referred to this ugly use of language as the "grotesque diction" of the satyr plays.[40]

Satyr plays were much shorter than the usual Greek fare, and, whereas tragedies were full of gloom and doom, the satyr play was designed to bring a little levity, sending theatre-goers home with a laugh, rather than a tear, for the human condition.

PLAYWRIGHTS OF ANCIENT GREECE

Chapter 5

Introduction

The four great Greek playwrights who were mentioned in Chapter 3 flourished in the fifth century BC, one after another with sometimes overlapping lives. They were Aeschylus (c. 425 - 455 BC), Sophocles (c. 497 – c. 405 BC), Euripides (480 BC – 405 BC), and Aristophanes (c. 450 – c. 388 BC). It was their remarkable talent that those who followed to designate their century as the Golden Age of Athens. The purpose of this chapter is to introduce you to these four foundational playwrights.

Aeschylus

To illustrate the influence of the tragic playwright Aeschylus, it is helpful to quote from a play by the comic playwright Aristophanes called *The Frogs* (apparently the Chorus members were costumed as frogs). He wrote the play one year after the death of Euripides and centers his play on the attempt of Dionysus, god of the theatre, to descend into Hades and restore Euripides to life so that Athens can continue to enjoy new plays. Upon the god's arrival, he discovers that Euripides and Aeschylus are spending their time in Hades fighting over which poet should have the honor of sitting at the right

**Aeschylus
b. 525 BC**

hand of Pluto. Although Aeschylus has spent the last fifty years next to Pluto, Euripides now argues that he is the better poet and deserves to be in the best seat, and so the two are going at each other as only two tragedians can. Dionysus decides to hold a contest of sorts in which Euripides and Aeschylus will compete to see which is worthy of "renewal." After a hilarious exchange in which Aeschylus succeeds in frustrating and one-upping Euripides, Dionysus decides to return with Aeschylus, who hollers over his shoulder, as he leaves, the Greek equivalent of, "Give my seat at the right hand of Pluto to Sophocles, not that impostor Euripides!"

In 405 BC when the play was written, these three great tragedians—Aeschylus, Sophocles, and Euripides—were all dead, and though Aristophanes may have thought he was free to kick them around on stage with impunity, he could not displace them in the history books. Still today, one cannot hear of fifth-century Greece without hearing their names, and each student of drama can decide which of them was the best.

Of the three Aeschylus was born first, so the improvements he made to the Greek theatre were well-established by the time Sophocles and later Euripides began to write, though that did not stop them from making their own innovations.

Information about Aeschylus' origins is scant. Biographers usually place his birth around 525 BC in Eleusis [ĭ-LÜ-sē-əs], a town twenty-seven miles northwest of Athens. His family was quite wealthy, and his father was a member of the nobility (called the *Eupatridae*, or "well-fathered," in Greek). Still, as a lad, Aeschylus would get his hands dirty by working in the vineyards—that is, at least, until he was visited in a dream by Dionysus, who told him to begin writing tragedies, a new art form at the time.

His first play was performed in 499 BC, when Aeschylus was twenty-six. However, he did not win a prize in the City Dionysia until he was almost forty. After that, he was a frequent winner until Sophocles appeared on the scene in 468 BC.

Corinthian helmet from the Battle of Marathon

Still, playwriting was not the only project that consumed Aeschylus' time as a young man. He was also a soldier and is known to have fought at the Battle of Marathon in 490 BC alongside his brother, who was killed. Ten years later he again fought the Persians, this time at the Battle of Salamis, a famous naval battle which saw the complete destruction of Xerxes' fleet. Again, Aeschylus succeeded in returning alive and whole, though this time his younger brother, Ameinius, lost a hand in the conflict. In 472 BC, Aeschylus wrote the only Greek play about the Battle of Salamis to have been written by a participant. Aptly named *The Persians*, the play centers on the theme of hubris, vaunting ego—the same vice referenced in Proverbs 16:18, "Pride goes before destruction, and a haughty spirit before a fall."

Can a playwright keep a secret, or is his desire to write riveting plays so strong that he is willing to shout secrets from the stage? This question arises from what happened after the induction of Aeschylus into the cult of the goddesses Demeter and Persephone, a secret society called the Eleusinian Mysteries. It was forbidden by penalty of death for members to reveal what actually went on at their gatherings. Now, one day Aeschylus was performing in one of his plays (unfortunately, its text has not survived), and when he delivered a line that appeared to reveal a secret of the cult, Eleusinian devotees who were in attendance at the play jumped onto the stage and attacked him. Brought before a tribunal on the charge of impiety, Aeschylus found himself surrounded by a mob who threatened to stone him on the spot. Order was restored only when his brother Ameinius, the wounded warrior, stepped forward, drew the crowd's attention to the stub of his arm, and pleaded Aeschylus' case on patriotic grounds. This, coupled with that ever-popular defense, "I didn't know it was wrong," earned the poet an acquittal.

The story of Aeschylus' death is legendary. It is said that one day, while Aeschylus was resting in the countryside, an eagle flew overhead, carrying in its talons a tortoise, which it desired to eat nearby. Seeing the bald head of the poet, the eagle mistook it for a rock and dropped the tortoise onto Aeschylus' head in an effort to crack the reptile's shell. Instead, apparently, it was the skull of Aeschylus that cracked.

The eagle, the tortoise, and Aeschylus

Sophocles

To understand Sophocles as a man, and not just as a dramatist, one must first understand the Greek concept of *paideia* (pī-DĀ-ə). Though the term is sometimes translated as "education," *paideia* was really the lifelong cultivation of knowledge and skills which would enable people to make a contribution to their *polis*, their city-state. Though there may not be an English equivalent of the word, the idea was at the root of President John F. Kennedy's famous exhortation: "My fellow Americans, ask not what your country can do for you, ask what you can do for your country."

Though born in Colonus in about 496 BC, Sophocles' *polis* was Athens, which allowed naturalized citizenship based upon the making of a benefaction, a payment or a significant service to the *polis*. Interestingly, Sophocles shows this exchange of benefaction for citizenship in his last play, *Oedipus at Colonus*. Oedipus, once king of Thebes but now an exile on the run from his enemies, explains to the king of Athens an oracle which had once foretold that the land where Oedipus was buried would be forever blessed. Oedipus, an old man nearing death, seeks citizenship in Athens with the promise that, upon his burial, Athens will have divine protection. These words show the response of the king:

Sophocles
c. 497 – c.405 BC

> Coming here, a suppliant to the gods,
> He pays full tribute to the State and me;
> His favors therefore never will I spurn,
> But grant him the full rights of citizen.[41]

Young Sophocles Leading the Chorus of Victory after the Battle of Salamis by John Talbott Donoghue, 1885

One way to view the many accomplishments of Sophocles, then, is to look at what he cultivated in himself in order to offer services to Athens. To do this, we must look at what was going on in his times in order to understand how Athens' situation offered him opportunities. To be specific, Sophocles was about five years old when the Greeks defeated the Persians at the Battle of Marathon in 490 BC. For the next ten years, Sophocles took his education, which included music, athletics, and dancing. Thus, in 480 BC, at the age of fifteen, he was prepared when history thrust him to the fore after the Battle of Salamis. Once again, the Greeks had defeated the Persians, and the city was in need of a talented lad to lead the boys' chorus in a *paean* (or hymn to the gods) as part of the city's victory celebration. They chose Sophocles. Following that, he continued to perfect his talents, and when he was twenty-seven, the Athenians awarded first prize to his play *Triptolemus* at the City Dionysia, where he beat out Aeschylus, the "reigning champion" of drama. Since Sophocles almost always acted in his own plays, we can conclude that he treated the Athenians to his own acting skills—perhaps in the role of Triptolemus, who (as we know from surviving fragments of the play) flew about on the stage "in his snakey chair."[42]   From these events of his youth, we can note that Sophocles' first service to his city was through his theatrical arts—music and drama.

As the years passed, Sophocles found additional ways to serve the *polis*. In 443 BC, he served as one of the *Hellenotamiai* (treasurers of Athens). Two years later, he was elected as one of the city's ten executive officials, and during the Samian War (440-439 BC), he served as a general and assisted in negotiations with the enemy. Age never seemed to stop him from desiring to serve. In 413 BC, at the age of eighty-four, he was elected as a *proboulos,* or commissioner, in which role he had to deal with the destruction of the Athenian army in Sicily during the Peloponnesian War.

In addition to being a dramatist, a soldier, and a city official for Athens, Sophocles played the role of priest as well. During the fifth century, the cult of the god Asclepius had been expanding in popularity. Now, Asclepius, the god of healing, was the son of Zeus, who served as one of the Muses, gods of the arts. Thus, Sophocles noticed the link Asclepius provided between health and the arts, understanding, as the playwright William Congreve put it centuries later, "Music hath charms to soothe the savage breast."[43]   As Robin Mitchell-Boyask, professor of classics at Temple University, has explained, "Sophocles came to be seen as Asclepius' sponsor in Athens. Festivals devoted to Asclepius thus became linked closely to two of the most important [dramatic] festivals in Athens"[44]—the Asclepieia and the City Dionysia. In 420 BC, when Sophocles set up an altar to Asclepius in his home, the Asclepieia festival was moved on the calendar to be performed on the eighth of Elaphebolion (a month corresponding to our March and April). This is notable since it was the day immediately preceding the City Dionysia and same day as the Proagon, a sort of contest-before-the-contest. Because of the link between Asclepius and Sophocles, it should come as no surprise that when the temple of Asclepius was erected on the Acropolis, it was placed adjacent to the theatre.

Rod of Asclepius

Sophocles wrote more than 120 tragedies and won the City Dionysia a record eighteen times. Only seven of his plays have survived in their entirety. Of these, the most famous are the Theban plays, which center around the ruling family of Thebes: *Oedipus Rex, Oedipus at Colonus*, and *Antigone*.[4]

---

[4] Though frequently referred to as a trilogy, the Theban plays were not composed as a set. Rather, each was one play in three different sets.

One of Sophocles' major contributions to the development of theatre was the addition of a third actor. This de-emphasized the narration role of the Greek Chorus and allowed for the development of more complex plots.

As an educated man and a contemporary of Socrates, Sophocles would well have understood the use of Aristotelian logic, and his plays do certainly contain examples of what the Greeks called an *agon*—a conflict in which the protagonist and antagonist argue or debate with each another. One example appears in *Antigone*, where Antigone admits that, though she disobeyed the king's edict, she was obeying a higher law, the law of the gods. Creon, on the other hand, maintains that the law must be obeyed no matter what. (Perhaps Sophocles shows his sympathy for Antigone's stand when he slips a logical fallacy into Creon's argument: "Now verily I am no man, *she* is the man, if this victory shall rest with her, and bring no penalty."[45] Not everyone has perfect mastery of logic.)

There are three legends about the death of Sophocles, which occurred in 406 or 405 BC at the age of ninety or ninety-one. Some say he choked on a grape while enjoying a dramatic festival in Athens. Others say he collapsed and died while trying to recite a speech from *Antigone* without taking a breath. Still others say he died of happiness upon winning first prize at the Dionysia. Whatever the cause, however, the family found it difficult to bury Sophocles because at that time the hostile Spartans were occupying the area where his ancestral tombs were located. It is said that Dionysius appeared in a dream to the Spartan commander, Lycurgus, seeking a truce for the burial of the great man, which Lycurgus did allow. On his tomb was placed the statue of a Siren, the symbol of the power of poetry,[46] and, according to the poet Lobon of Argos, the inscription read: "I am concealing by this tomb Sophocles, who took first place in the tragic art, a most august figure."[47]

EXERCISE 5.1: Analyzing a Character of Sophocles

<u>Directions</u>: After reading the introduction to an excerpt from *Philoctetes* by Sophocles, read the monologue that follows. When finished, proceed to the questions, where you can analyze the character using GOTE.

INTRODUCTION: *Heracles, when near death, had asked to be burned on a funeral pyre while he was still alive. Philoctetes had agreed to do so and, in the bargain, was given Heracles' bow as a reward. Subsequently, en route to the Trojan War, Philoctetes trampled on sacred ground and, for this fault, was bitten on the foot by a snake. The wound became so putrid that Odysseus could not stand the smell and left Philoctetes alone on a desert island. It is now ten years later. Odysseus, having learned from a seer that Philoctetes and the bow of Heracles are needed to defeat the Trojans, Odysseus has returned to the island, taking with him Achilles' son, Neoptolemus. It is the lad's task to persuade Philoctetes to aid Odysseus in his hour of need, but, as one might expect, Philoctetes is bitter.*

Marble Slab Depicting Philoctetes

Excerpt from *Philoctetes*
By Sophocles

PHILOCTETES

Ah! The miserable pain! Ah! The agony!

The gods! The gods hate me so much that none of my suffering has reached my country. Greece knows nothing about it!

The beasts who have abandoned me here in this disgusting fashion are now laughing at me without a care, while this torture is growing and becoming more intolerable by the day!

Neoptolemos, my son! Son of the great Achilles! Perhaps you have heard of me. The man before you is the man who holds the bow and arrows of Heracles. I am Philoctetes, Poeas' son. The two sons of Atreus, Menelaos and Agamemnon, leaders of the Greek army and that Kephalonian king, king Odysseus, cruel and shameless men, all three, have abandoned me here!

Here, on this desolate island, dying from this horrible wound, inflicted by the tooth of a murderous snake.

They've brought their fleet here, my son, on their way from the island of Athena Chryse and here, on this deserted island, they've dropped me and then they left.

Abandoned me here with this unbearable agony.

After so much torture and so many battles with the hurling seas, I was exhausted and so I had fallen asleep in some rocky cavern by the shore. That made them very happy. They tossed some old rags and some crumbs for me and then they left.

May the Heavens repay them in kind!

Ah!

And, so, my son, how do you think I felt when I woke up? When I saw that they have gone and left me here?

Oh, the tears I shed then, my son! The groans! The wails I shouted at them as I saw their ships that brought me here, sailing away! They had all gone! All of them!

No one was left here to help me with my miserable pains. No one to soften those pains a little. I looked around and I saw and felt nothing but pain! Pain and more pain! Plenty of that, my son!

Time followed Time and after a while I saw that I had to fend for myself, all alone, under that solitary roof there.

As for my belly's needs, they are provided by this bow. Wild birds, which I shoot on the wing and then crawl all the way to where the arrow drops them in order to fetch them.

I crawl about and I drag my miserable foot to where they fall. All on my own. In winter, when the ground is covered with ice, I must struggle in agony to get myself a drink, or a piece of wood for a fire. All alone and in utter misery, I'd struggle to start a fire. No fire here before I came. With great pain, I scratched one stone onto another until the deeply hidden spark revealed itself. Fire, my saviour!

Look over there! That cave there and that fire, provide me with all my needs. All except a cure for this pain!

And now you must learn about this island, my boy!

No one comes to this island of his own free will. There's no harbour here. Nowhere to come and do any trade. No roof to spend the night. No sensible sailor will ever come here.

Of course, it can happen that someone might get here against his will. All sorts of things have happened in the race of mortals over their long history. Well, these sailors come, show a great deal of pity for me and sometimes they may even give me a bit of food or some clothing but, alas, no one but no one will ever listen to my pleas about taking me back home.

None of them will take me home!

No, my son. This is the tenth year now that I've been living here. A miserable existence. A slow death by hunger and torture and by this horrible disease that's as gluttonous as Hades himself!

And all this because of that ruffian, Odysseus and those Atreus brothers, Agamemnon and Menelaos! This is what they've done to me! This is how they've treated me!

May the gods of Olympus give them the same treatment![48]

1. What seems to be Philoctetes' goal?

2. What obstacle stands in his way?

3. What tactics does he use (or consider) in order to achieve his goal?

4. What degree of expectation does Philoctetes have that he can achieve his goal?

Euripides

From beginning to end, the life of Euripides was colorful. He was born to a woman who hawked vegetables in the streets of Athens, and he was killed, in the end, by wild dogs. At least, that is the beginning and the end that legend has attached to him.

Euripides
480 BC – 405 BC

What we know about Euripides comes mainly from some fragments of biographical text written by the chronicler Philochorus in the early third century BC and Satyrus in the second century BC. In addition, the introduction to a Byzantine collection of Euripides' plays contains a *Life* of Euripides, which drew on both of those sources. The fact that he hated women and may have had warts on his face can be gleaned from some references to him in comic plays, especially those of Aristophanes. With these things in mind, let's take a look at the famous Greek playwright, Euripides.

Euripides was born on the island of Salamis in 480 BC, on the same day, it is said, that the famous Battle of Salamis was raging between the Greeks and the Persians. While he was growing up, his father (Mnesarchus) was a shopkeeper in Athens, and his mother (Cleito) sold vegetables in the streets of the city, if legend is to be believed.

A Greek vase depicting pankration

(His critics poked fun of him for that and some today argue the story is not true, but, to most folks nowadays, having an enterprising mother is certainly no cause for disgrace.)

When Euripides was a small boy, his father learned from an oracle that his son was destined to receive awards in competitions, and though some say this was a prophecy about his later victories in theatrical competition, his father took it to mean that his son was going to need athletic training. Therefore, Euripides took training in boxing and even participated in ancient Greece's version of the Extreme Olympics—an event called *pankration* [see image], in which the only rules were that one could not bite his opponent or use his fingernails to gouge out his eyes, nose, or mouth.

But Euripides had an intellectual side as well, and he apparently concluded that the prophecy rendered in his childhood meant that he would win prizes from writing and performing in plays. To put it in twenty-first century terms, he decided that instead of "going for the gold" at the Olympics, he would try for an Oscar instead. Apparently, he did not underestimate himself, winning drama prizes at the 81st Olympiad and at the festivals of Dionysus a number of times. He was even awarded first prize several years after his death for plays which were not actually performed while he was still alive. Altogether, Euripides wrote a total of ninety-two plays—all tragedies, eighteen of which have survived. It is said that the philosopher Socrates even collaborated with him once on a play. Euripides was also a painter who achieved a standard high enough to have some of his works displayed in Megara, a town on the Attic coast across from the island of Salamis, his home.

In his own time (and until quite recently, in fact), Euripides was considered to be a woman-hater, a vice which those who knew him attributed to the fact that he was married twice, both times to women who cheated on him. However, many today look at his play about Medea, the legendary wife of Jason, as evidence that Euripides must have had a great understanding of and sympathy for "the lot of woman."

One anecdote about the playwright is that he often withdrew to a place on Salamis called now the Cave of Euripides, where he could be unbothered by the need to make small talk with folks he disliked and focus instead on the lofty thoughts of his tragic heroes and heroines. Because his writing often employs sea imagery, some believe his cave faced the sea. The play *Hecuba* is especially rife with sea imagery, as seen at the outset, when the ghost of Polydorus describes his murder at the hands of an assassin: "He . . . casts me into the briny flood. . . . Hence prostrate am I on the shore or heaving in the surge of the ocean by the many fore and back rollings of the billows unlamented, uninterred."[49]

Though he did not seem to get along well with his fellow Athenians, he was well-liked by foreigners, and near the end of his life settled in Magnesia in Thessaly. So popular was he with the authorities there that he was asked to serve as their *proxenos*, a kind of diplomat.

Molossian Hound

The manner of Euripides' death, though awful, seems oddly suited to a Greek tragedian with a sense of poetic justice. As the story goes, while Euripides was in Macedonia, a Molossian hound belonging to the king, Archelaus, got loose and wandered into a village, where it was captured, sacrificed to the gods, and eaten. For this outrage, the king levied a fine against the villagers. Knowing Euripides was respected by Archelaus, the villagers turned to him for help in their cause, which he apparently provided. One day at some time later, Euripides was resting under a tree in the Macedonian countryside unaware that Archelaus' dogs were out and about on a hunting expedition. When released, the hounds, seeing the poet resting under a tree, raced toward him, tore him to shreds, and ate him—truly a kind of poetic justice for dogs whose fellow hunter had been served up by Euripides' friends.

Aristophanes

Life

The first record we have of Aristophanes [ār-ə-STŎF-ə-nēz] is for the year 427 BC, when his first play won second prize at the City Dionysia. He later claimed that he was only eighteen when he won the prize, which would make his birth year around 445 or 446 BC. Born into a wealthy family, Aristophanes received a good education and would have become familiar with the great poets and playwrights who had preceded him. He is known to have composed thirty plays (all comedies with political and social satire), but only eleven of them have survived.

Aristophanes
c. 445 BC – 386 BC

A member of the generation that saw the end of Athens' Golden Age, Aristophanes—despite the wealthy family and the good education—was no stranger to hardship. He was about fourteen when the Peloponnesian War broke out and fifteen when the great plague afflicted Athens. These events, along with the starvation that resulted from Sparta's war-time destruction of Athenian crops, familiarized Aristophanes with suffering and death. One of his satirical plays, *Lysistrata*, is particularly concerned with the effect of what must have seemed a never-ending war to the wives awaiting their husbands' return from war. As Lysistrata saw it:

> [I]f the women join us
> From Peloponnesus and Boeotia, then
> Hand in hand we'll rescue Greece.[50]

The war did end in 404 BC after widespread starvation had brought Athens to its knees. In its triumph, Sparta suspended democracy in Athens, and the sarcastic political commentary of Aristophanes came to an end. He died in 380 BC.

Jokester or Bully?

Everybody likes a class clown, but when does "joking" turn into bullying? Aristophanes largely practiced the latter kind of humor—the mocking, ridiculing, bullying type. It is perhaps a testimony to the free speech and democracy of Athens that his biting satire was, for the most part, permitted to flourish.

In the end, though, would we say that Aristophanes was a jokester or a bully? To answer this, let us look particularly at his play entitled *The Clouds*, which mocked the philosopher Socrates as a truth bender with his head in the clouds. The Chorus in this play represents the inspiration of the philosophers, and

The *deus ex machina* lowering Socrates to the earth in Aristophanes' mocking play, *The Clouds*

early on Socrates is asked if they are "demi-goddesses." He replies, thus:

> SOCRATES
> Not at all. They are the Clouds of heaven, great goddesses for the lazy; to them
> we owe all, thoughts, speeches, trickery, roguery, boasting, lies, sagacity.

Later, after a passage delivered by the Chorus, this exchange appears:

> STREPSIADES
> Oh! Earth! What august utterances! How sacred! How wondrous!
>
> SOCRATES
> That is because these are the only goddesses; all the rest are pure myth.
>
> STREPSIADES
> But by the Earth! Is our father, Zeus, the Olympian, not a god?
>
> SOCRATES
> Zeus! What Zeus! Are you mad? There is no Zeus.[51]

Later in the play, after receiving instruction from Socrates, Strepsiades' son also becomes an atheist and, having learned how to construct deceitful arguments, argues that he owes his father no respect. In other words, Socrates has corrupted the lad.

Now, here we have two serious charges—atheism and corruption of the youth of Athens—the very charges for which Socrates was tried, found guilty, and executed. Plato, the student of Socrates, later wrote a *prosopopoeia* (speech-in-character) called the *Apology*, in which Socrates defends himself against his accusers. Near the beginning of the speech, we find this passage:

> And first, I have to reply to the older charges and to my first accusers, and then
> I will go to the later ones. For I have had many accusers, who accused me of
> old, and their false charges have continued during many years; and I am more
> afraid of them than of Anytus and his associates, who are dangerous, too, in
> their own way. But far more dangerous are these, who began when you were
> children, and took possession of your minds with their falsehoods, telling of
> one Socrates, a wise man, who speculated about the heaven above, and
> searched into the earth beneath, and made the worse appear the better cause.

These are the accusers whom I dread; for they are the circulators of this rumor, and their hearers are too apt to fancy that speculators of this sort do not believe in the gods. And they are many, and their charges against me are of ancient date, and they made them in days when you were impressible—in childhood, or perhaps in youth—and the cause when heard went by default, for there was none to answer. And, hardest of all, their names I do not know and cannot tell; unless in the chance of a *comic poet* (emphasis added).[52]

In short, Plato accuses Aristophanes of bringing about the trial and death of Socrates because of the way he presented the great man in a play. No doubt, Aristophanes would give the typical response, "But I was only joking!" Perhaps he was, but whether a joke is funny is determined not by the person who says it, but by the persons who hear it, and it does not appear from these words that Socrates and Plato were laughing.

Four hundred years later, the Roman writer Plutarch undertook to describe the comedies of Aristophanes:

[T]he witticisms of Aristophanes are bitter and rough and possess a sharpness which wounds and bites. And I do not know wherein his vaunted cleverness resides, whether in his words or his characters. Certainly even whatever he imitates he makes worse; for with him roguishness is not urbane but malicious, rusticity not simple but silly, facetiousness not playful but ridiculous, and love not joyous but licentious. For the fellow seems to have written his poetry, not for any decent person, but the indecent and wanton lines for the licentious, the slanderous and bitter passages for the envious and malicious.[53]

Even among the Romans of the early Empire, Aristophanes' bitter words left him with a tarnished reputation.

Old Comedy

The term *Old Comedy* refers to comic plays of Greece written in the fifth century BC. As with tragedy, the origin of comedy was in song, which can be seen by breaking down the Greek word *kōmōidía*, which combines *kōmos* ("revel") and *aoidiā* ("ode" or "song). Aristophanes is known as the father of comedy, and his plays provide good examples of Greece's Old Comedy.

First, it is important to understand that Greek comedy was not like the comedies of today. Rather than fun, wholesome entertainment, Aristophanes' comedies were biting satires directed at political figures, military leaders, philosophers, rival poets—and even the audience from time to time.

The person most frequently and bitterly attacked in the plays was the Athenian general Cleon, a rather cruel leader who was disliked by the aristocracy. But Cleon did take some revenge by bringing a lawsuit against Aristophanes for some wisecracks about Athens presented in his play *The Babylonians*. Apparently there were foreign dignitaries in the audience, and Cleon believed the play made Athens look small in their eyes, which was disadvantageous when Athens was leading them in war.

Plays in the tradition of old Comedy included song, dance, buffoonery, coarse language, and a lot of jokes involving body noises. The characters often included gods and heroes, though they were not usually treated reverently.

There were six parts of a play in the Old Comedy:

a. The introduction in which the subject matter of the play would be introduced

b. The *parados*, or entry of the Chorus

c. The *agon* [Ä-gŏn], or contest, in which two characters would engage in a debate

d. The *parabasis* [pä-RÄB-ə-sĭs], a speech by the Chorus which often heaped invective on powerful people

e. The use of farce, comic scenes involving the ridiculous

f. A final banquet or wedding

The era of Old Comedy produced such classics as *The Frogs* and *The Clouds*, but with the appearance of Menander in the late fourth century BC, New Comedy came into its own.

Menander

What can Egyptian mummies teach you about Greek plays? Quite a bit, it turns out, thanks to the thriftiness of the fellows who made the mummy cases in which they lay their dead. Fortunately, for us, these men knew the value of re-cycling and would use old books to make a *papier mâché* material called cartonnage, which they used to line

the mummy cases. In 1906, as archaeologists worked in the tombs of the Egyptians, they became curious about the origin of the papyri used to make the cartonnage and were amazed to discover that the Egyptians had used pages from nine works of the Greek comic playwright Menander (c. 342-290 BC). In 2003, another work by Menander turned up in recycled pages (called *palimpsests*) from the ninth century AD. Amazingly, all of these were still readable.

Menander
(c. 342 – 290 BC)

Menander was born about eighty-five years after the death of the first major comic writer, Aristophanes. His father Diopeithes is thought to be the man Demosthenes referred to as the Athenian general and governor of the Gallipoli peninsula in Turkey (known in antiquity as Thracian Chersones). Menander probably learned to enjoy comedy from his uncle Alexis, who was also a comic poet.

Menander authored 100 comedies, but, despite the fragments discovered in Egypt, only one play remains in its entirety—*The Grouch*, which concerns a grumpy father who does not want his (poor) daughter to marry the (rich) man she loves. Now that's a twist. Menander's first play, entitled *Anger*, had appeared in 321 BC. Five years later, *The Grouch* won a prize at a festival, and a year after that Menander had a victory at the City Dionysia.

The companion of several important persons, Menander was supported financially by a man who has made all the history books—Ptolemy I Soter. Ptolemy had been a Macedonian general under Alexander the Great, who made him ruler of Egypt. (There Ptolemy founded the dynasty which ended, regrettably, with Cleopatra.) Any chance those Egyptian mummy cases were made from Ptolemy's books?

Menander was a great observer of human nature and left us many maxims in his works. One of the most famous was, "Evil communications corrupt good morals." Menander's sound judgment is displayed in the following excerpt from *The Grouch*, when the young Sostratos tries to persuade his father Kallippides to allow him and his sister to marry siblings from a poor family:

KALLIPPIDES
I don't want to take on a bride and a bridegroom who are both beggars: one is enough for us.

SOSTRATOS
You're talking about money, an unstable business.
If you think that all of this will stay with you
for all time, guard it, share with no one
what you own. But what you're not yourself master of
—and everything you have is not yours but luck's—
don't begrudge any of these things, father, to anyone.
For luck herself will take everything of yours for herself
and assign them again to someone else, perhaps someone who
doesn't deserve it.[54]

Looking "through a glass darkly," as Paul put it, how close Menander came to a teaching of the Old Testament: "The LORD gave, and the LORD has taken away; blessed be the name of the LORD" (Job 1:21b).

With such a sense of morality, it is easy to understand why Greek educators in the pre-Christian period collected Menander's sayings into a book and used them to teach morals in their schools.

Menander drowned in 290 BC while swimming in the harbor of Piraeus, where he had a villa. His friends built for him a tomb on the road to Athens near the monument to the memory of Euripides.

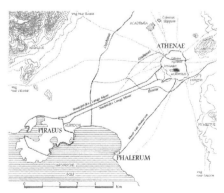

The road between Piraeus and Athens

EXERCISE 5.2: Primary Sources

<u>Directions</u>: Please read the two excerpts below which comment on the talent of Menander and then answer the questions that follow.

Excerpt from *Institutes of Oratory*
By Quintilian

Now, the careful study of Menander alone would, in my opinion, be sufficient to develop all those qualities with the production of which my present work is concerned; so perfect is his representation of actual life, so rich is his power of invention and his gift of style, so perfectly does he adapt himself to every kind of circumstance, character and emotion[55] (10.1).

Excerpt from *Moralia*
By Plutarch

Moralia by Plutarch, 1531

He [Menander] has made his poetry, of all the beautiful works Greece has produced, the most generally accepted subject in theatres, in discussions, and at banquets, for readings, for instruction, and for dramatic competitions. For he shows, indeed, what the essence and nature of skill in the use of language really are, approaching all subjects with a persuasiveness from which there is no escape, and controlling every sound and meaning which the Greek language affords. For what reason, in fact, is it truly worthwhile for an educated man to go to the theatre, except to enjoy Menander? And when else are theatres filled with men of learning, if a comic character has been brought upon the stage?[56]

1. For what reasons did Quintilian believe that Menander alone could teach his students all they needed to know about oratory?

   a.

   b.

c.

2. Plutarch states Menander's poetry was the most generally accepted of all Greek works in all venues. What reasons does he give for this accomplishment?

    a.

    b.

    c.

3. Plutarch ends with two rhetorical questions. In your own words, state what point he is trying to make.

New Comedy

While Aristophanes is the best examples of the tradition of Old Comedy, Menander is the best example for New Comedy, which began in 320 BC and continued until the mid-200's BC. Gone were the gods, the superheroes, and the biting political satire. The new emphasis was on ordinary people in ordinary situations—what today we call *situation comedy*. To present these situations, New Comedy had a set of *stock characters*—stereotypes that appear again and again in the plays from the period. Some of the stock characters were these:

- the angry old man

- the cunning slave

- the boasting soldier

- the penny pincher

- the sly merchant

- the absent-minded fellow

- the fault-finder

- the parasite (person who receives dinner invitations through false flattery)

New Comedy continued to develop in the Roman period and was revived in the Renaissance by playwrights such as William Shakespeare. European drama continued to include plays of the New Comedy type into the eighteenth century, and, of course, today's plays, movies, and television programs also owe a debt to the comic style of Menander.

COSTUMES, PROPS, AND MASKS

Chapter 6

Introduction

Drama coaches go to great lengths to find ways for students to understand the character they are to represent onstage. No doubt, more than one student has been asked to, "Be the tree!" or "Be the beast!"—all in an effort to get the actor into the "mind" of an inanimate or non-human character. However, in ancient Greece, the religious beliefs of the actors were such that they believed actors actually did become the person represented by their costume and mask. Dionysius was sometimes called the god of "ecstasy," one definition of which is "standing outside oneself." Since Dionysius was also the god of the theatre, an actor could easily believe that he would stand outside himself and accept the identity of the character he was portraying. But what were the costumes and masks that these actors wore, and did they use props to make their transformation believable?

Costumes

The various garments of everyday Greeks and Romans would have served as costumes in some scenes, just as they would today. The basic item would be the *chiton* (a robe or tunic), the *himation* (a garment worn over the chiton), the *chlamys* (short cloak), and the *peplos* (gown).

The woman at left wears a chiton. The other two wear a himation over a chiton.

Kothurnoi (buskins)

Footwear included the *kothurnus* (an open-toed shoe with calf-high laces), worn by characters in a tragedy, and the *soccus* (a soft, low-heeled slipper) worn by characters in a comedy. Typically, the word *kothurnus* is translated into English as *buskin*, which may derive from the Middle Dutch word *brosekin*, which meant "small leather boot."

Perhaps the best way to discover what costumes were used in Greek and Roman plays is to examine various scripts to see what garments are mentioned in the dialogue. For example, look at these lines of Orestes from *The Choephori* by Aeschylus:

> What sight is yonder? what this woman-throng
> Hitherward coming, by their sable garb
> Made manifest as mourners?[57]

A woman in a
peplos

From this, we can conclude that the Chorus and the actress playing Electra, who enter almost immediately, were clothed in black (sable).

One play where costumes are central to the plot is Aristophanes' comedy *The Frogs*. The god Dionysius, who is a character in this play, appears at the door of his brother Heracles, who greets him with these words:

> I vow I can't help laughing, I can't help it.
> A lion's hide upon a yellow silk,
> A club and buskin! What's it all about?
> Where were you going?[58]

Now, the attire described here is the typical garb of Heracles, and, in answer to his brother's question, Dionysius explains that he, along with his slave Xanthias, will descend into Hades to bring back Euripides, who had died a year before the play was written. However, things get crazy when the two actually arrive at their destination, and most of the play's humor results from mistaken identity. First, Dionysius is mistaken for Heracles, which presents a problem since the character who "recognizes" him wants revenge for some affront. When Xanthias mocks Dionysius for being afraid of the avenger, Dionysius makes this suggestion:

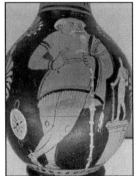

> Come then, if you're so very brave a man,
> Will you be I, and take the hero's club
> And lion's skin, since you're so monstrous plucky?
> And I'll be now the slave, and bear the luggage.[59]

A vase showing the character Xanthias eyeing a statue of Heracles

They actually swap garments and accoutrements three times onstage, not difficult since the lion's hide would have been draped across the shoulder. Each time there is a costume swap, another comic scene ensues. One has to wonder just how easy (or difficult) it was for the *himatiomisthês* (costumer) to come by a lion's hide!

EXERCISE 6.1: Costumes as Spectacle

Statue of Darius I
By Fabien Dany
www.fabiendany.com.

Directions: Imagine you are the *himatiomisthes* (costumer) for the Greek stage. Read each selection from a Greek play and indicate, in the space provided, what would be required to costume the actor(s).

1. In *The Persians* by Aeschylus, the Chorus invokes the ghost of Darius the Great to rise from Hades, describing him thus:

    CHORUS
    King, our king of old, come forth, draw near! Rise to the barrow's topmost point, lift your saffron-dyed sandal, display the crest of your royal tiara! Come forth, O blameless father Darius.[60]

    Another translator, instead of referring to Darius' "sandal," called it "thy *sock* in saffron dyed," suggesting the *soccus*, or soft slipper.

    a. Looking at the footwear shown in the image of Darius' statue, what kind of shoes would you line up (or make) for the actor playing the part—a sandal or a slipper?

    b. What color is saffron?

2. In *The Suppliant Maidens* by Aeschylus, the King of Argos enters to welcome a group of maidens, whose lines are recited by a women's Chorus, thus:

> PELASGUS, KING OF ARGOS
>
> From where comes this band we address, clothed in foreign attire and luxuriating in closely-woven and barbaric robes? For your apparel is not that of the women of Argos, nor yet of any part of Hellas. How you have gained courage thus fearlessly to come to this land, unheralded and friendless and without guides, this makes me wonder. And yet, truly, I see that branches usually carried by suppliants are laid by your side before the gods assembled here—as to this alone can Hellas guess with confidence.[61]

 a. What would be the Greek costumer's biggest challenges in attaining or creating the attire for the maidens in this scene?

 b. What props have the maidens entered with and laid down?

Props

The prop master in ancient Greece was called the *skeupoios*. It is known that the skene originated as a storehouse of props, and it is possible to figure out what soe of them were by scanning the dialogue of the plays for clues.

For example, the lines from *The Frogs*, quoted above, reveal not only the costume ("a lion's hide upon a yellow silk"), but also the props ("a club" for Dionysus and "luggage" for Xanthius). Similarly, in *The Persians,* Darius arises from the tomb with not only his yellow slippers, but a "tiara." These give us a glimpse into the stage properties, or props, that would probably have been stored in the skene.

In most orchestras at the theatre, as we have seen, the architects had installed a permanent altar, or *thymele*. This was sometimes employed as a prop.[62] In fact, in *The Children of Heracles* by Euripides, the plot revolves around the old man Iolaus who is hiding the orphans of Heracles at the altar of the temple of Zeus:

IOLAUS:
But being bereft of all Greece, coming to Marathon and the country under the same rule, we sit suppliants at the *altars* of the gods, that they may assist us[63] (emphasis added).

Iolaus receives the protection of the king, Demphon, who makes this declaration:

DEMOPHON:
Three ways of misfortune urge me, O Iolaus, not to reject these suppliants. The greatest, Jupiter, at whose altars you sit, having this procession of youths with you; and my relationship to them, and because I am bound of old that they should fare well at my hands, in gratitude to their father; and the disgrace, which one ought exceedingly to regard. For if I permitted this altar to be violated by force by a strange man, I shall not seem to inhabit a free country.[64]

But beyond the components of the theatre itself, what props may have been required? The script of *Helen* by Euripides provides some suggestions. Look at this passage spoken by Theonoe as she enters with her handmaids, for example:

THEONOE:
Lead on, bearing before me blazing brands, and, as sacred rites ordain, purge with incense every cranny of the air, that I may breathe heaven's breath free from taint; meanwhile do thou, in case the tread of unclean feet have soiled the path, wave the cleansing flame above it, and brandish the torch in front, that I may pass upon my way.[65]

Winged Victory (Nike) with an incense burner

Here we see burning torches, incense, and, by implication, a censer. Later in the play, Menelaus, who is determined to keep Helen from Theoclymenus, presents a soliloquy in which his use of the pronoun *this* suggests props the audience would have been able to see:

- "Old king *beneath this tomb of stone* reposing, pay back thy trust!"

- "I am resolved to slay Helen, and then to plunge *this two-edged sword* through my own heart."

- "And our two corpses will be lying side by side *upon this polished slab*, a source of deathless grief to thee, and to thy sire reproach."

Even animals were used in this play, as Theoclymenus at one point enters with his hunting dogs and nets.

In the final scene, King Menelaus, disguised as a "messenger," tricks Theoclymenus into thinking that he died at sea and that Helen must sail out to perform the funeral rites of her "dead" husband. Of course, he plans to attend Helen in this escape plan. To perform the funeral rites according to Greek custom, he tells Theoclymenus they will need bronze weapons and an "empty bier" which is "decked," probably with flowers. All these items are brought to Menelaus and Helen, and they head offstage in the direction of the ships that Theoclymenus (the poor dupe) has provided.

EXERCISE 6.2: Props as Spectacle

<u>Directions</u>: The following scene is from Euripides' play *Iphigenia in Aulis*. Clytemnestra has just arrived in Aulis. Read the excerpt from the dialogue and then answer the questions that follow.

CHORUS
Behold Iphigenia, the king's royal child, and Clytemnestra, the daughter of Tyndareus; how proud their lineage! how high their pinnacle of fortune! These mighty ones, whom wealth attends, are very gods in the eyes of less favoured folk.

Halt we here, maidens of Chalcis, and lift the queen from her chariot to the ground without stumbling, supporting her gently in our arms, with kind intent, that the renowned daughter of Agamemnon but just arrived may feel no fear; strangers ourselves, avoid we aught [anything] that may disturb or frighten the strangers from Argos. (*Enter CLYTEMNESTRA and IPHIGENIA.*)

CLYTEMNESTRA

I take this as a lucky omen, thy kindness and auspicious greeting, and have good hope that it is to a happy marriage I conduct the bride. (To Attendants) Take from the chariot the dowry I am bringing for my daughter and convey it within with careful heed.

My daughter, leave the horse-drawn car, planting thy faltering footstep delicately. (To the CHORUS) Maidens, take her in your arms and lift her from the chariot, and let one of you give me the support of her hand, that I may quit my seat in the carriage with fitting grace.

Some of you stand at the horses' heads; for the horse has a timid eye, easily frightened; here take this child Orestes, son of Agamemnon, babe as he still is.

What! sleeping, little one, tired out by thy ride in the chariot? Awake to bless thy sister's wedding; for thou, my gallant boy, shalt get by this marriage a kinsman gallant as thyself, the Nereid's godlike offspring. Come hither to thy mother, my daughter, Iphigenia, and seat thyself beside me, and stationed near show my happiness to these strangers; yes, come hither and welcome the sire thou lovest so dearly.[66]

5th-century BC sarcophagus from Amathus, Cypress, depicting chariots

1. This scene requires the entrance of a chariot. Was there one or more than one horse drawing the chariot?

2. Write the names of the people who were conveyed in the vehicle to this scene?

3. Is there another, un-named person whose presence is implied?

4. In addition to the passengers, what else was in the chariot?

5. Consider these questions about performing the chariot scene:

   a. What was the condition of Orestes upon arrival?

   b. If you were to perform this play, what would you do about the horses?

   c. If you put on this play, how might you construct the chariot, assuming that you would probably want to reveal the passengers and cargo gradually, as the lines require? (You can either write a description or draw a sketch.)

EXERCISE 6.3: Becoming the *Skeupoios* for Props

Directions: Imagine you are the *skeuopoios* (prop-master) for the Greek theatre. Read each scene. Then, in the space provided, indicate what props you would need to gather for the actors.

1. In the play *Agamemnon* by Aeschylus, Clytemenestra welcomes her husband home from the Trojan War with these lines:

> CLYTEMENESTRA:
> And now, I pray you, my dear lord, dismount from your car, but do not set on common earth the foot, my King, that has trampled upon Ilium. [*To her attendants*] Why this loitering, women, to whom I have assigned the task to strew with tapestries the place where he shall go? Quick! With purple let his path be strewn, that Justice may usher him into a home he never hoped to see.[67]

   a. What prop is required for this scene?

   b. What color was requested, and why do you think that color was particularly named?

   c. What clue suggests the size of the tapestries?

2. In the same play, a Chorus masked as old men (long-ago warriors) deliver these lines:

> CHORUS
> But we, incapable of service by reason of our aged frame, discarded from that martial mustering of long ago, wait here at home, supporting on our canes a strength like a child's. For just as the vigor of youth, leaping up within the breast, is like that of old age, since the war-god is not in his place; so extreme age, its leaves already withering, goes its way on triple feet, and, no better than a child, wanders, a dream that is dreamed by day.[68]

   a. What prop, mentioned in the first sentence, would each member of the Chorus need here?

b. What phrase in the last sentence also references a person with this prop? Explain your answer.

Masks

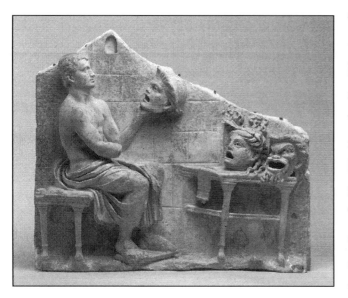

The Roman poet Menander with masks from New Comedy): youth, false maiden, old man.

The closest we can come to a Greek theatre mask in our own times would be the head piece of a college mascot's costume. In other words, it was large and cumbersome, but necessary in order for the character to be visible to the spectators in the most remote section of the cavea. The mask also had the effect of completely transforming the identity of the actor, which was important when each of the three actors was playing multiple roles.

Materials for mask-making in ancient times included wood, clay, linen, leather, cork, and sometimes human hair. The purpose of the masks was to identify the gender, age, social status, and personality of the various characters. In the second-century AD, a Greek scholar named Julius Pollux wrote a book in which he listed and described forty-four masks that were needed for the particular character types required for the Greek (and Roman) stage. Keeping in mind that the theatres in the ancient world usually lacked scenery, one can see how important the masks were to what Aristotle called the spectacle of the play.

In his discussion of the spectacle (special effects) of the theatre, Aristotle referred to the *skeuopoios* (prop maker), and though he placed spectacle last in his list of theatre elements, he nevertheless acknowledged that it "had an emotional attraction of its own."[69] From the list of Pollux, one can see how this was so—as Pollux used words like *common, cruel, horrid, rustic,* and *delicate* to describe the visage presented by each mask.

Pollux' list also breaks masks down by gender, age, social class, and dramatic genre (tragedy or comedy), as the following excerpts indicate.

Old Man Tragic Masks

With respect to masks, the tragic might be a smooth-faced man, a white, grizzled, black-haired, flaxen, more flaxen, all of them old: and the smooth-faced oldest of these; having very white locks, and the hairs lying upon the prominence. By prominence I mean the upper part of the countenance rising above the forehead in the shape of the Greek λ [lambda]. With respect to beards, the *smooth-faced* should be very closely shaven and have thin, lantern jaws. The *white-haired* is all hoary with bushy locks about the head, has an ample beard, jutting eyebrows, and the complexion almost white, but the prominence short. The *frizzled* denotes the hoary hairs to be a mixture of black and grey. But the *black-haired*, deriving his name from the colour, has a curled beard and hair, rough face, and large prominence. The *flaxen* has yellowish bushy hair, lesser prominence, and is fresh colored. The *more flaxen* has a sameness with the other, but is rather more pale to represent sick persons.[70]

Mosaic depicting a theatre mask from Sousse, Tunisia

Young Men's Tragic Masks

The *young men's* masks are the common, curled, more curled, graceful, horrid, second horrid, pale, less pale. The *common* is eldest of the young men, beardless, fresh-colored, swarthy, having locks clustering, and black. The *curled* is yellow, blustering, with bushy hair encompassing a plump face, has arched eyebrows, and a fierce aspect. The *more curled* differs in nothing from the former, but in being a little younger. The *graceful* has hyacinthian locks, fair skin, is lively, and of a pleasant countenance, fit for a beautiful Apollo. The *horrid* is robust, grim-visaged, sullen, deformed, yellow-haired. The yellow-haired attendant. The *second horrid* is so much more slender than the former, as he is younger; and an attendant. The *pale* is meager, with disheveled hair, and of such a sickly countenance as is suitable for a ghost, or wounded person. The *less pale* is entirely like the common in every other respect except that it is made pale on purpose to express a sick man, or a lover.

Slaves' Tragic Masks

The *slaves' masks* are the leathern, peaked beard, flat-nose. The *leathern* having no prominence, has a fillet, and long white hairs, a pale whitish visage, and rough nostrils, a high crown, stern eyes; the beard a little pale, and looks older than his years. But the *peaked-beard* is in the vigor of life, has a high and broad prominence dented all round, is yellow-haired, rough, ruddy, and suited to a messenger. The *flat-nose* is bluff, yellow headed, the locks hang on each side from the forelock; he is beardless, ruddy, and likewise delivers a message.

Women's Tragic Masks

The *women's masks* are a hoary [whitish-gray] disheveled, a freed old woman, an old domestic, a middle-aged, a leathern, a pale disheveled, a pale middle-aged, a shaven maiden, second shaven maiden, a girl. The *hoary disheveled,* surpassing the rest, both in years and dignity, has white locks, a moderate prominence, is inclinable to paleness, and was anciently called the delicate. The freed old woman is of a tawny complexion and hoariness, having a small prominence; the tresses to the shoulders denote misfortune. The *old domestic*, instead of prominence has a fillet of lamb's wool, and a wrinkled skin. But the *middle-aged domestic* has a short prominence, and white skin, is grey haired, but not quite hoary. The *leathern*, younger than her, and has not any prominence. The *pale disheveled* has black hair, a dejected countenance, and her name from the color. But the *pale middle aged* is like the disheveled, except where she is shaven. But the *shaven maiden* instead of prominence wears a smooth-combed tate [tuft of hair], is shaven almost quite round, and of a color inclinable to paleness. And the *other shaven maiden* is perfectly like her, but without the tate and curls, as if she had been often in misfortunes. The *girl* is a juvenile mask, such as Danae might have been, or any other virgin.

Attendant Tragic Masks

The *attendant masks* are an horned Aetaean, a blind Phineus or Thamyris, one having a blue eye, the other a black; a many-eyed Argus, or Tyro with livid cheeks, as in Sophocles, which she shattered from the blows of a cruel stepmother; or Euippe, Chiron's daughter, changed into a horse in Euripides: or Achilles disheveled for *Patroclus*, an amymone, a river, mountain, Gorgon, Justice, Death, a Fury, Madness, Guilt, Injury, Centaur, Titan, Giant, Indian, Triton; perhaps, also a City, Priam, Persuasion, the Muses, Hours, Nymphs of Mithaeus, Pleiades, Deceit, Drunkenness, Idleness, Envy; which latter might likewise be comic masks.

Satyr Masks

Satyric masks are a hoary satyr, bearded satyr, beardless satyr, Grandfather Silenus. The other masks are all alike, unless where the names themselves show a peculiar distinction, as the Father Silenus has a more savage appearance.

Old Men's Comic Masks

But those of the new were a first grandfather, a second grandfather, governor, long-bearded, or shaking old man, Ermoneus [beloved], peaked-beard, Lycomodeus, procurer, second Ermoneus, all of them old. The *first grandfather* oldest, close-shaven, having very pleasant eyebrows, an ample beard, lantern jaws, dim sight, white skin, comely face, and forehead. The *other grandfather* is more slender, sharper-sighted, morose, of a pale complexion, has an ample beard, red hair, cropped ears. The *governor*, an old man, with a crown of hairs round his head, stooping, broad-faced, and has his right eyebrow elevated. But the long-bearded, *shaking old man*, has a crown of hairs round his head, an ample beard, no elevation of eyebrows, dimmer sight. *Ermoneus* has a bald crown, ample beard, elevated eyebrows, sharp sight. The *procurer* resembles Lycomodeus in other respects, but has distorted lips, and contracted eyebrows; and either a bald crown or pate. The *second Ermoneus* is shaven and has a peaked beard. But *peaked-beard* has a bald crown, elevated eyebrows, sharp chin, and is morose. *Lycomodeus* has curled beard, long chin, and extends one eyebrow representing curiosity.

Young Men's Comic Masks

The *young men's masks* are a common young man, a black young man, a curled young man, a delicate, rustic, threatening, second flatterer, parasite [moocher], a fancied mask, Sicilian. The *common* is ruddy, athletic, swarthy, having few wrinkles upon his forehead, and a crown of hairs, with elevated eyebrows. The *black young man* is younger, with depressed eyebrows, like an educated and accomplished youth. The *curled young man* is handsome, young, ruddy, has his name from his hairs, his eyebrows extended, and one wrinkle on his forehead. But the *delicate young man* is haired like the common and youngest of all, fair,

educated in the nursery, showing delicacy. The *rustic* is weather-beaten, broad-lipped, flat-nosed, and has a crown of hairs. But the *threatening young man*, who is a soldier, and braggart, of black complexion and tresses, his hairs shaking like the other threatener, who is more tender and yellow haired. The *flatterer* and *parasite* are black, quite unpolished, cringing, sympathizing. The parasite's ears are more bruised, and he is more pleasant; and the flatterer's eyebrows are disagreeably extended. But the *fancied mask* has cheeks bored and chin shaven, is superbly dressed, and a foreigner: But the *Sicilian* is a third parasite.

Slaves' Comic Masks

The *slaves' comic masks* are a grandfather, upper slave, thin-haired behind, or bristly slave, a curled slave, a middle slave, foppish slave, shaking upper slave. The *grandfather* alone of all the slaves is hoary, and shows the freed-man. But the *upper slave* wears a crown of red hairs, elevates the eyebrows, contracts the forehead, and among slaves is like an aged governor among freed-men. But the *thin*, or *bristly haired*, has a bald crown, red hairs, and elevated eyebrows. The *curled slave* has curled hairs, but they are red, as is likewise his color; he has a bald crown and distorted face, with two or three black curls, and the same on his chin; the *shaking upper slave*, like the upper, except in the hairs.

Women's Comic Masks

The *women's masks* are a thin old woman, or harlot; a fat old woman, a domestic old woman, either sedentary or active. The *harlot* is tall, with many small wrinkles, fair, palish, and with rolling eyes. The *fat old woman* has many wrinkles on a plump skin and a fillet round her hair. The *domestic old woman* is flat-faced and in her upper jaw has two axle teeth and on each side one. The *young women's masks* are a talkative, curled maiden, demi-rep, second demi-rep, hoary-talkative, concubine, common woman of the streets, beautiful courtesan, golden harlot, lampadion, maiden slave, slattern. The *talkative* has full hair smoothed a little, high eyebrows, fair skin. The *curled maiden* has a distinction of false hair, high eyebrows, and black; and a pale whiteness in her skin. The *demi-rep* has a white skin, and her hair tied behind in a knot, would be thought a brie.

The *second demi-rep* is known by the distinction of her hair only. The *hoary talkative* indicates her person by the name, she shows the harlot left off trade. The *concubine* resembles her, but is full haired. The *common woman-of-the-streets* is higher colored than the demi-rep, and has curls round her ears. The *courtesan* has least finery, and her head bound with a fillet. The *golden harlot* has much gold upon her hair. The *mitred harlot* has her head bound with a variegated mitre. *Lampadion* has her hair platted in the form of a lamp. The *maiden slave* wears only a short white frock. The *slattern* is distinguished by her hair, and is both squat and being dressed in a red gown, waits upon the courtesans.

ACTIVITY 6A: Mask Making

Directions: The purpose of this activity is to provide you the opportunity of making a theatre mask. The checklist below is designed to help you brainstorm ideas and suggest materials.

- ✓ For the foundation of your mask, you can purchase an unpainted plastic mask from a hobby store or make a mask from *papier maché*.

- ✓ Decide whether you'll make a full mask or a partial mask (such as the mask employed in *The Phantom of the Opera*).

✓ Consider whether you will make a comic mask or a tragic mask.

✓ Assemble supplies such as hot glue and scissors.

✓ Use paints or markers to create features.

✓ Adorn the mask with materials such as fabric, yarn, ribbon, etc.

✓ Where appropriate, include elements of nature such as flowers, feathers, ivy, leaves, stars, moons, etc.

✓ Use color and design to create a mood: angry, sad, etc.

✓ Employ features such as hair, beards, warts, and tears.

✓ Choose a character type: kings or queens, heroes, villains, young persons, old persons, fantasy characters, animals, etc.

THE RHETORIC OF GREEK PLAYS

Chapter 7

Introduction

Though we might refer to the great authors of antiquity as "ancient Greeks," there was a time when they were schoolboys being educated in the manner now called "the classical way." As part of early education in Greece, young people were taught to write using the *progymnasmata* [pro-goom-NÄZ-mə-tə], that is, the early exercises which prepare students for advanced rhetoric. By the time these great authors wrote their plays, they were, of course, remarkably skilled, but one can still perceive in their works the underlying elements that they learned when young.

Speech in Character (*Prosopopoeia*)

In the case of a dramatist, one can see a key progymnasmata element fundamental to plays: the speech-in-character (or *prosopopoeia*). While learning this element, the students would be asked to create characters and place them in tough situations. Then, in order to ensure the students would produce a believable speech for the character, the teachers asked the students to think in the way the character would think and speak in the way the character would speak. You can imagine how this would not always be easy. If I am a boy, how can I think of what a girl would say? If

I am young, how can I think of what an old person would say? The task pushes students to broaden their horizons about the human condition while, at the same time, steering them away from stereotypes.

The speech itself normally contained three parts, each using a different verb tense. First, the speaker would use present tense to explain his or her situation. Second, the speaker would slip into past tense (or present perfect tense) to explain how this situation came about. Last, the speaker would begin to talk about the future, perhaps expressing hopes, wishes, or fears. Such thoughts might well be expressed with future tense forms (*will, can, could, should, might, be going to*, etc.), but often (in English) such thoughts are expressed with a present tense verb followed by an infinitive (e.g., *hope to, wish to, want to, need to*, etc.) As they direct their thoughts to solving their problems, the speakers reveal their character. Will they handle their problems in a moral and ethical way, or will they strike out—hurting or even killing the one whom they perceive as the source of their problem?

Now, in a play, these speeches can appear in two different forms. One is the **soliloquy**, in which the speaker is alone (or *solo*) on the stage, speaking in a manner that will reveal his or her thoughts to the audience. The other is the **monologue**, in which the character addresses others on the stage.

In the exercises that follow, you will have a chance to examine the basic plot lines of some of the most famous Greek plays. Please examine each from the perspective of the progymnasmata element, speech-in-character, or *prosopopoeia*.

EXERCISE 7.1: Speech-in-Character in *Medea*

In the play *Medea*, Euripides composed a speech-in-character in the form of a monologue in which Medea pours out her heart about her awful plight. Here is the situation in which Medea finds herself: She is married to Jason, the hero of the story *Jason and the Golden Fleece*, and together they have two children. However, Jason has recently decided to set her aside and marry another woman. Filled with anger and hate, Medea steps forward to speak to the women of Corinth about her situation. Read the speech, paying attention as you read to the three parts of a speech-in-character: *present problem* + *past cause* + *future resolution*. When finished, answer the questions that follow.

From *Medea*
By Euripides

Klara Zeigler as
Medea

MEDEA: (1) From the house I have come forth, Corinthian ladies, for fear lest you be blaming me; (2) for well I know that amongst men many by showing pride have gotten them an ill name and a reputation for indifference, both those who shun men's gaze and those who move amid the stranger crowd, and likewise they who choose a quiet walk in life. (3) For there is no just discernment in the eyes of men, for they, or ever they have surely learnt their neighbour's heart, loathe him at first sight, though never wronged by him; and so a stranger most of all should adopt a city's views; nor do I commend that citizen, who, in the stubbornness of his heart, from churlishness resents the city's will.

(4) But on me hath fallen this unforeseen disaster, and sapped my life; (5) ruined I am, (6) and long to resign the boon of existence, kind friends, and die. (7) For he who was all the world to me, as well thou knowest, hath turned out the worst of men, my own husband. (8) Of all things that have life and sense we women are the most hapless creatures; (9) first must we buy a husband at a great price, and o'er ourselves a tyrant set which is an evil worse than the first; and herein lies the most important issue, whether our choice be good or bad. (10) For divorce is not honourable to women, nor can we disown our lords. (11) Next must the wife, coming as she does to ways and customs new, since she hath not learnt the lesson in her home, have a diviner's eye to see how best to treat the partner of her life. (12) If haply we perform these tasks with thoroughness and tact, and the husband live with us, without resenting the yoke, our life is a happy one; if not, 'twere best to die. (13) But when a man is vexed with what he finds indoors, he goeth forth and rids his soul of its disgust, betaking him to some friend or comrade of like age; whilst we must needs regard his single self.

(14) And yet they say we live secure at home, while they are at the wars, with their sorry reasoning, for I would gladly take my stand in battle array three

times o'er, than once give birth. (15) But enough! this language suits not thee as it does me; (16) thou hast a city here, a father's house, some joy in life, and friends to share thy thoughts, but I am destitute, without a city, and therefore scorned by my husband, a captive I from a foreign shore, with no mother, brother, or kinsman in whom to find a new haven of refuge from this calamity. (17) Wherefore, this one boon and only this I wish to win from thee,—thy silence, if haply I can some way or means devise to avenge me on my husband for this cruel treatment, and on the man who gave to him his daughter, and on her who is his wife. (18) For though woman be timorous enough in all else, and as regards courage, a coward at the mere sight of steel, yet in the moment she finds her honour wronged, no heart is filled with deadlier thoughts than hers.[71]

Questions:

1. In the space below, write the numbers of the sentences that describe Medea's present situation, including her reflections on the lot of women, in general.

2. In the space below, write the number of the sentence that explains what happened (or has happened) in the past to cause the problem.

3. In the space below, write the number of the sentence that explains what Medea is planning to do in the future.

4. What does Medea's speech reveal about her emotional state and her personality?

EXERCISE 7.2: Speech-in-Character in *Antigone*

INTRODUCTION: Another famous Greek play is Antigone by Sophocles. Though written first, it stands as second in a trilogy called The Theban Plays. The understood background of the play is the tragedy of King Oedipus, who was fated by an oracle to kill his father and marry his mother, Jocasta. Despite everyone's best efforts to prevent this from happening, it did happen, and years later, after the birth of four children, Oedipus and Jocasta rail against their fate. Jocasta kills herself, and Oedipus gouges out his eyes. In the opening scene, two sisters—Ismene (ĭs-MĀN-ē) and Antigone (ăn-TĬG-ə-nē)—are discussing what has now happened to two brothers—Eteocles (ĭ-TĒ-ə-klēz) and Polynices (pŏl-ə-NĪ-sēz). Specifically, we learn the brothers have killed each other fighting over which of them would be king of Thebes (Eteocles, the younger of the two, currently holds sway there). The two brothers no longer an obstacle, an ally of Eteocles by the name of Creon has now become king, and, we learn, is not treating the corpses of the two brothers with equal respect. Eteocles has been buried honorably, but the body of Polynices is to remain unburied. Creon's plan is calculated to deter future troublemakers, who will now see Polynices' body being mauled by animals and decaying in view of all. Moreover, Creon has decreed death as the punishment for anyone who might bury Polynices. Antigone is outraged by such treatment and is determined to give her brother a decent burial no matter what the consequences. She asks Ismene to help her. What follows is the dialogue between the two.

<u>Directions</u>: Please begin by reading the two brief speeches, both of which have the earmarks of *prosopopoeia*. As you read, keep in mind the stages of a speech-in-character (*present problem + past cause + future resolution*). Then answer the questions that follow.

Excerpt from *Antigone*
By Sophocles

ISMENE
Bethink thee, sister, of our father's fate,
Abhorred, dishonored, self-convinced of sin,
Blinded, himself his executioner.
Think of his mother-wife (ill sorted names)
Done by a noose herself had twined to death   5
And last, our hapless brethren in one day,
Both in a mutual destiny involved,
Self-slaughtered, both the slayer and the slain.
Bethink thee, sister, we are left alone;
Shall we not perish wretchedest of all,   10
If in defiance of the law we cross
A monarch's will?—weak women, think of that,
Not framed by nature to contend with men.

Remember this too that the stronger rules;
We must obey his orders, these or worse.   15
Therefore I plead compulsion and entreat
The dead to pardon. I perforce obey
The powers that be. 'Tis foolishness, I ween,
To overstep in aught the golden mean.

ANTIGONE
I urge no more; nay, wert thou willing still,   20
I would not welcome such a fellowship.
Go thine own way; myself will bury him.
How sweet to die in such employ, to rest,—
Sister and brother linked in love's embrace—
A sinless sinner, banned awhile on earth,   25
But by the dead commended; and with them
I shall abide for ever. As for thee,
Scorn, if thou wilt, the eternal laws of Heaven.[72]

Questions:

1. In Lines 1-8, what past events does Ismene review for her sister, events which greatly affect their present situation?

2. In Line 9, how does Ismene describe their present situation?

3. In Lines 10-19, what does Ismene say they must do?

4. In Lines 20-22a, what emotion seems to have come over Antigone; in other words, what is her present emotional condition?

5. The rest of Antigone's speech focuses on the future.

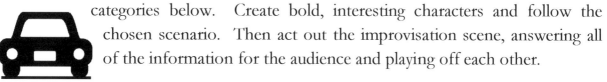

   a. In Line 22b, what does Antigone say she is going to do?

   b. In Lines 23-27a, what does Antigone predict will be the ultimate result of her action?

   c. In Lines 27b-28, what does she tell Ismene to do?

   d. If you were performing the role of Antigone, what tone of voice would you use to deliver that line to Ismene? Explain your answer.

ACTIVITY: Speech-in-Character Improvisation

<u>Directions</u>: Set up four chairs as if they were the front and back seats of a car. They should face the class. Pick four students, one to be the driver and the other three to be the passengers. Choose a scenario: for example, they are on their way to Disney World, they are driving from Alaska to Florida, they are on their way to the hospital, etc. Take a few minutes to create a character by answering questions from the three categories below. Create bold, interesting characters and follow the chosen scenario. Then act out the improvisation scene, answering all of the information for the audience and playing off each other.

Note: When doing "improv," it is only natural that someone will say or do something silly or something that might not make sense. This is not a problem. It is a natural part of the learning process. Actors have to be willing to stretch themselves and try new things, or they will never grow in their rhetoric skills. It is helpful to keep in mind the teaching of 1 Thessalonians 5:11, which exhorts us to "encourage one another and build one another up."

1. **Information about the past**

   <u>Examples</u>: Where are you from? What was your childhood like? Tell a funny/sad story about your past. Explain why you are on the way to your destination. What has happened to make the trip necessary/desirable?

2. **Information about the present**

   <u>Examples</u>: What kind of car are you in? What are the road conditions? Who are your fellow passengers? Besides the other passengers, what else is in the car? What are you irritated/excited/worried about, etc.? What are you thinking about right now? What are you afraid/hopeful of? You have an incoming cell phone call. What does the caller say?

3. **Information about the future**

   <u>Examples</u>: What are you going to do when you arrive at your destination? What may happen as a result of your action? What does the future hold for you? What are you going to do tomorrow?

Invective (*Psogos*)

Another element of the progymnasmata, which the great playwrights would have learned in school, was invective (*psogos*). In this exercise, students learned how to go about the sometimes necessary task of public blame or censure, as in the case of an evildoer or a tyrant. Invective was a mainstay in Old Comedy since much of Greek comedy centers on satire of public figures and even the gods. It can also be found in tragedies where, for example, the protagonist might light into the antagonist with a litany of complaints about his or her evil character and evil deeds.

A "textbook" invective would have five major components: (a) the person's family background; (b) the person's education, including the names of persons who had influenced him or her in a bad way; (c) the person's vices (disrespect, cruelty, etc.); (d) the person's evil deeds (lying, murder, etc.); and (e) comparison, showing how the person is similar to another, well-known evil figure. These would have been the rhetorical arrows in the dramatist's quiver.

In a play, of course, dramatists would adapt the invective to the events surrounding its delivery. That is to say, one does not always find all five of the components in a dramatic invective. In the exercise below, you will have a chance to examine an invective from another play by Sophocles entitled *Electra*.

EXERCISE 7.3: Invective in *Electra*

INTRODUCTION: *The title character of Sophocles' play Electra is the daughter of King Agamemnon, hero of the Trojan war, and his wife Clytemnestra. When Agamemnon had returned from the war seven years before the action of the play, he had brought with him a concubine named Cassandra. This betrayal greatly incensed Clytemnestra, even though Clytenestra herself had taken a lover, Aegisthus, during the king's absence. Clytemnestra and Aegisthus have now murdered Agamemnon and Cassandra, and Aegisthus has assumed the kingship, taking Clytemnestra as his wife. Electra, At the beginning of the play, Electra is lamenting that her brother, Orestes, is not there to help her avenge her father's murder. (Concerned for the safety of her brother, she had helped the lad escape to Phocis.) When her mother enters, Electra does not hide her hatred and*

berates Clytemnestra for murdering her own husband. Clytemnestra justifies her crime by saying that she was only taking revenge for Agamemnon's sacrifice of their daughter Iphigenia before the war. Electra asks leave to speak freely and launches into an invective against her mother.

<u>Directions</u>: Please read the invective, keeping in mind the elements of an invective. When finished reading, answer the questions that follow.

Excerpt from *Electra*
By Sophocles

ELECTRA

Hear, then! Thou ownest, with unblushing face,
Thyself a murdress. What could be more base
Than this confession? For though well or ill
Death were deserved, 't is thy dishonor still.
But that a villain's tongue persuaded thee   5
To do this act of shameless perfidy,
And that there was no justice in the deed,
I now can show thee, if thou wilt but heed.
Go, ask the huntress, Dian, for what wrong
The winds at Aulis kept the Greeks so long;   10
Or, since from that pure goddess no reply,
May come to such as thou, I'll tell thee why,
'T was thus: My father once, in sylvan chase,
Struck down a stag near Dian's dwelling-place—
The very grove wherein her altar stood—   15
And dyed the sacred herbage with its blood.
But this enraged Latona's daughter so
That she forbade the ocean winds to blow,
And seaward-bound detained the mighty host,
With idle prows high ranged along the coast,   20
Till, for the profanation to atone,
Their chief should offer up his dearest one.
The impatient army, eager to be free,
Forced him to give his child unwillingly.
Thus, not for Menelaus did she die;   25

But, since by this thou hopest to justify,
Thine act, suppose it for a moment so—
What right had'st thou to deal the avenging blow?
When did the gods this power on thee confer,
Creating thee the furies' minister?   30
Beware lest thou, ordaining such a course,
Feel not thyself its all-destroying force.
For if we thus may life for life decree,
The hand of vengeance first should fall on thee.
But tell me, in requital for what ill,   35
Doest thou consort with the assassin still?
Why still his every idle wish obey,
And for his sake thy children cast away?
Hopest then some evil haply to redress,
By a continuous life of shamelessness?   40
Or that it may assuage thy daughter's woe,
To see thee wedded to our deadliest foe?
But why advise thee, or attempt to teach,
Whose every word is of my slanderous speech
To my own mother? Such I count not thee,   45
In whom is less of love than tyranny.
For what a life of sorrows I endure,
Controlled by thee, and by thy paramour;
While sad Orestes, rescued from thy hand,
Wears out existence in a foreign land.   50
And him thou has accused me, oftentime,
Of training an avenger of thy crime.
This I had done, and my revenge secured,
Had I had power—of this be well assured.
Denounce me, if thou wilt, for such intent,   55
To all the world, as false and insolent;
For though it proves me treacherous and base,
To thy example I am no disgrace.

Questions:

1. **Vices:** Electra makes reference to Clytemnestra's evil character traits (vices) that lie at the bottom of her sins. What fault of character is suggested in Lines 1 and 6 by the phrases "unblushing face" and "shameless perfidy"?

2. **Evil Influences:** To what evil influence does Electra refer in Line 5 when she mentions "a villain's tongue"?

3. **Evil Deeds:** What seven evil deeds does Clytemnestra lay at her mother's feet in these lines? (You may want to refer to the introduction to the excerpt.)

   a. Line 6

   b. Lines 28-30

   c. Line 36

   d. Line 38

   e. Lines 47-48

   f. Lines 49-50

4. **Comparison:** Lines 7-25 of the invective can be considered the comparison feature of invective.

   a. By way of comparison to her mother's act of murder, how does Electra characterize Agamemnon's "murder" of Electra's sister?

   b. Who comes out the better in the comparison?

Encomium (Enkômion)

Whereas the purpose of invective is to blame, the purpose of encomium is to praise. In praise of a person, the speakers giving praise would turn the topics of invective to the positive. That is to say, instead of vices, they would speak of virtues. Instead of evil deeds, good deeds. Instead of evil influences, good influences. Comparison would be made with widely esteemed figures in history who influenced the world in similar ways, or perhaps to lesser figures who did not show the fortitude or integrity of the favored person.

Yet people were not the only subjects of encomia. Not infrequently in great dramatic works, one finds a speech praising a hero or heroine, a god or goddess, a place, or an animal. Perhaps one of the most praised of all animals in Greek literature was Bucephalus, the horse of Alexander the Great. Pliny, Plutarch, Diodorus, Arrian, Ptolemy, and Sicullus have all sung the praises of the gallant steed.[73] What is more, Stephen Pressfield in his novel *The Virtues of War*, has Alexander deliver a eulogy for Bucephalus after the Battle of the Hydaspes. This eulogy is an excellent model of an encomium to an animal written in our own vernacular.[74]

An encomium could also be written about a city, which becomes logical in Greek culture if one recalls that in ancient times the the Greeks lived in city-states, not nations. Just as in our time, each nation has its national anthem, in ancient Greece the poets would sing the praises of their cities. In his handbook on the progymnasmata, Hermogenes of Tarsus (AD 161-180) listed numerous topics which the writers or orators might use to praise their cities: "You will speak about its origin (saying) that its people are autochthonous [sprung from the earth], and about its growth, how it was nurtured by gods, and about education, how the people have been taught by the gods. And you will examine, as in the case of a man, what sort of manners the city has, what sort of institutions, what pursuits it follows, what it has accomplished."[75]

In the exercise below, you will have the opportunity to examine an encomium to Athens that appears in Sophocles' play *Oedipus at Colonus*.

EXERCISE 7.4: Encomium to a City in *Oedipus at Colonus*

INTRODUCTION: Oedipus at Colonus *was the last play of the Theban plays written by Sophocles, but the action of the play is actually second. (In today's parlance, it might be called a prequel to* Antigone.*) In the first part of the trilogy, we are introduced to Oedipus, who grew up not knowing that he was the son of Laius, king of Thebes, and his queen, Jocasta. Laius had once been told the prophecy that his son would kill him and marry Jocasta. Determined to avert such a horrible fate, Laius left young Oedipus in the wild to be devoured by beasts, but a shepherd and his wife pitied him and took him in. When grown to manhood, Oedipus gets wind of the prophecy, and believing that his foster parents are his actual parents, leaves home so that the prophecy cannot be fulfilled. On his way, he encounters a man who tries to kill him; Oedipus strikes back, killing him, not realizing the man was his father. Through a series of events, Oedipus is made king and marries Jocasta, not knowing that she is his own mother. Together they have four children—two sons (Polynices and Eteocles) and two daughters (Antigone and Ismene). When Oedipus finally figures out the prophecy was actually fulfilled and that he has committed patricide and incest, he puts out his own eyes, and Jocasta commits suicide. He is cast out of Thebes. In* Oedipus at Colonus, *Oedipus (now old and, of course, blind) arrives with Antigone in Athens and begs mercy of King Theseus to harbor him. While awaiting the king's reply, the Chorus steps forward and presents a paean of praise (an encomium) to Athens.*

Directions: Please read the excerpt below, keeping in mind the elements of an encomium. When finished reading, answer the questions that follow.

Excerpt from *Oedipus at Colonus*
By Sophocles

CHORUS

strophe 1

Thou hast come to a steed-famed land for rest,
O stranger worn with toil,
To a land of all lands the goodliest
Colonus's glistening soil.
'Tis the haunt of the clear-voiced nightingale,   5
Who hid in her bower, among
The wine-dark ivy that wreathes the vale,
Trilleth her ceaseless song;
And she loves, where the clustering berries nod
O'er a sunless, windless glade,   10
The spot by no mortal footstep trod,
The pleasance kept for the Bacchic god,
Where he holds each night his revels wild
With the nymphs who fostered the lusty child.

antistrophe 1

And fed each morn by the pearly dew   15
The starred narcissi shine,
And a wreath with the crocus's golden hue
For the Mother and Daughter twine.
And never the sleepless fountains cease
That feed Cephisus's stream,   20
But they swell earth's bosom with quick increase,
And their wave hath a crystal gleam.
And the Muses' quire will never disdain
To visit this heaven-favored plain,
Nor the Cyprian queen of the golden rein.   25

strophe 2

And here there grows, unpruned, untamed,
Terror to enemy's spear,
A tree in Asian soil unnamed,
By Pelops' Dorian isle unclaimed,
Self-nurtured year by year;   30
'Tis the grey-leaved olive that feeds our boys;
Nor youth nor withering age destroys
The plant that the Olive Planter tends
And the Grey-eyed Goddess herself defends.

antistrophe 2

Yet another gift, of all gifts the most   35
Prized by our fatherland, we boast —
The might of the horse, the might of the sea;
Our fame, Poseidon, we owe to thee,
Son of Kronos, our king divine,
Who in these highways first didst fit   40
For the mouth of horses the iron bit;
Thou too hast taught us to fashion meet
For the arm of the rower the oar-blade fleet,
Swift as the Nereids' hundred feet
As they dance along the brine.[76]   45

Questions:

NOTE: You may want to use colored ink or highlighters to mark the following references:

1. Underline references to gods, goddesses, and heaven.

2. Underline references to the natural beauty of the area.

3. Underline references to animals mentioned in the encomium.

4. Underline references to the beauty of music.

5. Underline references to the prospering people.

6. Underline the reference to the city's defense.

7. EXTRA CREDIT: If time permits, use the library or the Internet to identify the various gods and goddesses who are named.

Refutation (*Anaskeuê*)

Rhetoric has been defined as the art of persuasion. One of the tools of persuasion is the skill of refutation, that is, proving how it is that someone's version of events is false. Along with its companion, confirmation, wherein the speaker strives to prove a version of events to be true, refutation is famously employed in criminal trials, both the defense and the prosecuting attorney working from the same set of facts but coming up with completely different interpretations of the facts. There are four basic approaches available to the persons who are trying to confirm or refute a narrative. That is to say, they ask if the narrative is possible, probable, clear, and consistent—or *not*. Then, depending on the circumstances, two additional approaches may be used: Is the narrative expedient (advantageous) and appropriate—or *not*?

In the exercise below, you will have the opportunity to examine a refutation that appears near the end of Euripides' play *Hecuba.*

EXERCISE 7.5: Refutation in *Hecuba*

INTRODUCTION: *Written c. 424 BC, Euripides' play entitled* Hecuba *is a tragedy set in the aftermath of the Trojan War when the victorious Greeks, led by their king, Agamemnon, are still in Troy. Hecuba, queen of the fallen Trojan king, Priam, has not only lost her city and her husband to the Greeks, but she has also lost her son Polydore—not to the enemy, but to an ally—Polymestor, king of Thrace. Polydore had been sent to Thrace for safekeeping and had taken with him a part of the Trojan treasury. However, learning of the defeat of Troy, Polymestor had killed Polydore and stolen the treasure. The play centers on Hecuba's revenge against Polymestor. The excerpt below is an exchange between Polymestor and Hecuba as the two try to justify their evil deeds to Agamemnon. Polymestor begins with two narratives: first, his murder of Polydore and, subsequently, Hecuba's revenge upon him. Then Hecuba launches into a strong refutation of Polydore's version of events, putting the lie to his claim.*

Directions: Please read the excerpt below, keeping in mind the elements of a refutation. When finished reading, answer the questions that follow.

Excerpt from *Hecuba*
By Euripides

POLYMESTOR'S NARRATIVE

[A] I will tell my tale. There was a son of Priam, Polydorus, the youngest, a child by Hecuba, whom his father Priam sent to me from Troy to bring up in my halls, suspecting no doubt the fall of Troy. Him I slew; but hear my reason for so doing, to show how cleverly and wisely I had planned. My fear was that if that child were left to be thy enemy, he would re-people Troy and settle it afresh; and the Achaeans [Greeks], knowing that a son of Priam survived, might bring another expedition against the Phrygian land and harry and lay waste these plains of Thrace hereafter, for the neighbours of Troy to experience the very troubles we were lately suffering, O king.

[B] Now Hecuba, having discovered the death of her son, brought me hither on this pretext, saying she would tell me of hidden treasure stored up in Ilium by the race of Priam; and she led me apart with my children into the tent, that none but I might hear her news. So I sat me down on a couch in their midst to rest; for there were many of the Trojan maidens seated there, some on my right hand, some on my left, as it had been beside a friend; and they were praising the weaving of our Thracian handiwork, looking at this robe as they held it up to the light; meantime others examined my Thracian spear and so stripped me of the protection of both. And those that were young mothers were dandling my children in their arms, with loud admiration, as they passed them on from hand to hand to remove them far from their father; and then after their smooth speeches (wouldst thou believe it?) in an instant snatching daggers from some secret place in their dress they stab my children; whilst others, like foes, seized me hand and foot; and if I tried to raise my head, anxious to help my babes, they would clutch me by the hair; while if I stirred my hands, I could do nothing, poor wretch! for the numbers of the women. At last they wrought a fearful deed, worse than what had gone before; for they took their brooches and stabbed the pupils of my hapless eyes, making them gush with blood, and then fled through the chambers; up I sprang like a wild beast in pursuit of the shameless murderesses, searching along each wall with hunter's care, dealing buffets, spreading ruin. This then is what I have suffered because of my zeal for thee, O Agamemnon, for slaying an enemy of thine. But to spare thee a lengthy speech; if any of the men of former times have spoken ill of women, if any doth so now, or shall do so hereafter, all this in one short sentence will say; for neither land or sea produces a race so pestilent, as whosoever hath had to do with them knows full well.

HECUBA'S REFUTATION:

[C] Never ought words to have outweighed deeds in this world, Agamemnon. No! if a man's deeds had been good, so should his words have been; if, on the other hand, evil, his words should have betrayed their unsoundness, instead of its being possible at times to give a fair complexion to injustice. There are, 'tis true, clever persons, who have made a science of this, but their cleverness cannot last forever; a miserable end awaits them; none ever yet escaped. This is a warning I give thee at the outset.

[D] Now will I turn to this fellow, and will give thee thy answer, thou who sayest it was to save Achaea [Greece] double toil and for Agamemnon's sake that thou didst slay my son. Nay, villain, in the first place how could the barbarian race ever be friends with Hellas? Impossible, ever.

[E] Again, what interest hadst thou to further by thy zeal? was it to form some marriage, or on the score of kin, or, prithee, why? or was it likely that they would sail hither again and destroy thy country's crops? Whom dost thou expect to persuade into believing that? Wouldst thou but speak the truth, it was the gold that slew my son, and thy greedy spirit.

[F] Now tell me this; why, when Troy was victorious, when her ramparts still stood round her, when Priam was alive, and Hector's warring prospered, why didst thou not, if thou wert really minded to do Agamemnon a service, then slay the child, for thou hadst him in thy palace 'neath thy care, or bring him with thee alive to the Argives [Greeks]? Instead of this, when our sun was set and the smoke of our city showed it was in the enemy's power, thou didst murder the guest who had come to thy hearth.

[G] Furthermore, to prove thy villainy, hear this; if thou wert really a friend to those Achaeans, thou shouldst have brought the gold, which thou sayst thou art keeping not for thyself but for Agamemnon, and given it to them, for they were in need and had endured a long exile from their native land. Whereas not even now canst thou bring thyself to part with it, but persistest in keeping it in thy palace.

[H] Again, hadst thou kept my son safe and sound, as thy duty was, a fair renown would have been thy reward, for it is in trouble's hour that the good most clearly show their friendship; though prosperity of itself in every case finds friends. Wert thou in need of money and he prosperous, that son of mine would have been as a mighty treasure for thee to draw upon; but now thou hast him no longer to be thy friend, and the benefit of the gold is gone from thee, thy children too are dead, and thyself art in this sorry plight.

[I] To thee, Agamemnon, I say, if thou help this man, thou wilt show thy worthlessness; for thou wilt be serving one devoid of honour or piety, a stranger to the claims of good faith, a wicked host; while I shall say thou delightest in evil-doers, being such an one thyself; but I rail not at my masters.[77]

Questions:

1. First, examine Polymestor's narrative.

    a. Part A: Why did he kill Polydore?

    b. Part B: How did Hecuba take her revenge?

2. Now examine Hecuba's refutation.

    a. Part C: Speaking to Agamemnon about words and justice, what does Hecuba say is POSSIBLE for someone like Polymestor to do at times? Explain her point in your own words.

    b. Part D: In what way, according to Hecuba, is Polymestor's explanation about helping out the Greeks IMPOSSIBLE to believe? Answer in your own words.

    c. Part E: According to Hecuba, what is IMPROBABLE (i.e., not likely) about Polymestor's explanation of his actions? Answer in your own words.

    d. Part F: According to Hecuba, how are Polymestor's words INCONSISTENT with his actions? Answer in your own words.

    e. Part G: Hecuba thinks Polymestor's show of friendship for the Greeks is IMPROBABLE for what reason? Answer in your own words.

f. Part H: According to Hecuba, in what way was Polymestor's murder of Polydore INEXPEDIENT to himself? Answer in your own words.

g. Part I: When she addresses Agamemnon, what does Hecuba say would be INAPPROPRIATE for a king? Answer in your own words.

Description of Action (*Ekphrasis*)

Description (*ekphrasis*) is another of the progymnasmata exercises, but the rhetoric teachers created specific approaches for different types of description. Approaches would vary depending on whether one was describing a person, a place, an object, time, or action.

To describe action, students were given the following approaches: motion, speed, force, and direction. Especially key to the description of action is the selection of the verb.

- For **motion**, would the subject be strolling, creeping, leaping, limping, or frolicking?

- For **speed**, would the subject be racing, crawling, marching, or waddling?

- For **force**, would the subject be crashing, thrashing, whipping, or simply stroking?

- For **direction**, adjectives and adverbs become prominent.

  o One might refer to the directions north, south, east, and west.

  o One might refer to three-dimensional directions, such as upward, downward, backwards, or sideways.

o One might also employ adverbial prepositional phrases such as *to the sea* or *into the heavens*.

In the exercise below, you will have the opportunity to examine a description of action that appears at the end of *Prometheus Bound* by Aeschylus.

EXERCISE 7.6: Description of Action in *Prometheus Bound*

INTRODUCTION: At the outset, we should take note of the fact, although the play Prometheus Bound *was long attributed to Aeschylus (c. 525-455 BC), some scholars now believe it was the work of a dramatist writing in about 415 BC. However, since it is nearly impossible to prove the authorship one way or the other, in this textbook tradition will be followed, and the author will be identified as Aeschylus.*

The play is based on the mythological Greek god Prometheus (prō-MĒ-thē-əs), who was punished by Zeus for bringing humans the gift of fire, a gift which made the arts and sciences possible. His punishment was to be tied (or bound, as the title puts it) to a rock on a mountaintop for a period of thirteen generations. Through the course of the play, Prometheus is visited not only by the Chorus, but also by the god Oceanus and the maiden Io. He boldly speaks of the future demise of Zeus, which so angers Zeus that he sends Hermes (messenger of the gods) to extract from Prometheus any details he has concerning the rebellion against him. Prometheus refuses, so Zeus causes an earthquake and sends a thunderbolt in order to plunge Prometheus into an abyss.

The final speech in the play is that of Prometheus, whose words reveal Aeschylus' skill at Description of Action. It is interesting to note how different translators have rendered the passage into English. Below you will find three versions, appearing alphabetically by author: the first is by G. M. Cookson; the second, by Walter Headlam; the third, by Henry David Thoreau.

<u>Directions</u>: Begin by reading the three translations. Then, using the chart that follows, work with a partner to discuss the translations, trying to reach a consensus as to which is the best overall translation, according to the principles of Description of Action: motion, speed, force, and direction. When finished, share your decision with your classmates. Be ready to explain your choice.

Excerpt from *Prometheus Bound*

I. By G. M. Cookson

PROMETHEUS

The time is past for words: earth quakes
Sensibly: hark! pent thunder rakes
The depths, with bellowing din
Of echoes rolling ever nigh-er:
Lightnings shake out their locks of fire;
The dust cones dance and spin;
The skipping winds, as if possessed
By faction—north, south, east and west,
Puff at each other; sea
And sky are shook together: Lo
The swing and fury of the blow
Wherewith Zeus smiteth me
Sweepeth apace, and visibly,
To strike my heart with fear. See, see,
Earth, awful Mother! Air,
That shedd'st from the revolving sky
On all the light they see thee by,
What bitter wrongs I bear![78]

II. By Walter Headlam

PROMETHEUS

Ah now in deed, in word no more, the earth is rocked and the subterranean
sound of thunder is booming at my side, the fiery streaks of lightning flashing
out, and whirlwinds, rolling up the eddying dust; the blasts of all the winds leap
wildly and display contention setting contrary against each other, and the sky is
confounded with the sea: So dire the rushing onset that proceeds from Zeus
against me manifestly working terror. O thou holy one, my Mother, O thou

Sky, revolving the common light of all the world, beholdest thou the injustice I am suffering?[79]

By Henry David Thoreau

PROMETHEUS
Surely indeed, and no more in word,
Earth is shaken;
And a hoarse sound of thunder
Bellows near; and wreathes of lightning
Flash out fiercely blazing, and whirlwinds dust
Whirl up; and leap the blasts
Of all winds, 'gainst one another
Blowing in opposite array;
And air with sea is mingled;
Such impulse against me from Zeus
Producing fear, doth plainly come.
O revered Mother, O Ether
Revolving common light to all,
You see me, how unjust things I endure.[80]

.Element	Anonymous	Headlam	Thoreau
1 **Force** **(Quake)**	Earth quakes / Sensibly.	The earth is rocked.	Earth is shaken.
2 **Force** **(Thunder)**	Pent thunder rakes / The depths, with bellowing din / Of echoes rolling ever nigh-er.	The subterranean sound of thunder is booming at my side.	A hoarse sound of thunder / Bellows near.
3 **Direction** **(Lightning)**	Lightnings shake out their locks of fire.	The fiery streaks of lightning flashing out. . . .	Wreathes of lightning / Flash out fiercely blazing.
4 **Motion** **Direction** **(Dust)**	The dust cones dance and spin.	Whirlwinds, rolling up the eddying dust	Whirlwinds dust / Whirl up. [*sic*]
5 **Direction** **(Winds)**	The skipping winds, as if possessed/By faction— north, south, east and west,/Puff at each other	The blasts of all the winds leap wildly and display contention setting contrary against each other	[Whirlwinds] leap the blasts / Of all winds, 'gainst one another / Blowing in opposite array.
6 **Force** **(Sea/Sky)**	Sea / And sky are shook together.	The sky is confounded with the sea	And air with sea is mingled.
7 **Force** **(Zeus' Slap)**	The swing and fury of the blow / Wherewith Zeus smiteth me / Sweepeth apace, and visibly, / To strike my heart with fear.	So dire the rushing onset that proceeds from Zeus against me manifestly working terror	Such impulse against me from Zeus / Producing fear, doth plainly come.

GREEK THEATRE TIDBITS FROM PRIMARY SOURCES

Chapter 8

Introduction

The theatres in Greece were massive structures, and from time to time one reads of ways they were used by politicians and generals in the great sweep of history. The sections below provide some examples of just such events in ancient Athens.

Pericles and the Theatre in Athens

The period when the great dramatists were producing their plays has come to be known as the Golden Age of Athens (480 BC – 404 BC). However, it was also the time when Pericles came to prominence in Athens and left his mark on the city so such a degree that the period of his leadership (c. 460 BC – 429 BC) has come to be called the Age of Pericles. A great statesman, orator, and general, Pericles had a great love of the theatre. In fact, the first time his name appears in the public record of Athens is in 472 BC when he served as the *choregus* (funder) for the performance of *The Persians* by Aeschylus.

**Pericles of Athens
c. 495-429 BC**

When Pericles first began his rise to power, he was in competition with older men who had already made a name for themselves. One of these was Cimon [SĪ-mən; Greek, KĒ-män], a general who had distinguished himself at the Battle of Salamis. Generally speaking, Cimon favored the aristocracy, but he did not ignore the poor altogether:

> [Because of his wealth, Cimon] was enabled to take care of the poor, inviting every day some one or other of the citizens that was in want to supper, and bestowing clothes on the aged people, and breaking down the hedges and

enclosures of his grounds, that all that would might freely gather what fruit they pleased.[81]

If he were to compete with Cimon, Pericles would have to find a way also to make himself popular among the common folk, so perhaps moved by his own passion for the theatre, he decided that, among other benefits he bestowed on them, they would be provided with free admission to the plays. Later, the Roman historian Plutarch took a cynical view of this gesture, saying that Pericles had improved his political position because he had "bought the people over, what with moneys allowed for shows."[82]

Aware of the often immoral themes of the mimes, Plutarch had another objection:

> Many say, that by him, the common people were first encouraged and led on to such evils as appropriations of subject territory, allowances for attending theatres, payments for performing public duties, and by these bad habits were, under the influence of his public measures, changed from a sober, thrifty people that maintained themselves by their own labors, to lovers of expense, intemperance, and license.[83]

Apparently, emotions run so deep about the relationship between politicians and the poor that the critics even pursue the politicians beyond the grave. The British patron of the arts George Lyttelton, 1st Baron Lyttelton, was still hammering Pericles in 1760 when he wrote a fictional dialogue in which the ghost of Cosimo de Medici, a ruler of medieval Florence who died in 1464, scolds the ghost of Pericles, who died in 429 BC:

> Yet I have heard you condemned, for rendering the people less sober and modest, by giving them a share of the conquered lands, and paying them wages for their necessary attendance in the public assemblies and other civil functions; but more especially for the vast and superfluous expense you entailed on the state in the theatrical spectacles with which you entertained them at the cost of the public.[84]

Self-serving, ill-advised or generous—Pericles loved the theatre and enabled the poor people to enjoy it along with the rest of the Athenians. His motives are left for students of history to debate.

Another way in which Pericles influenced the theatre is that he established the first *odeon*, which was a smaller theatre for the presentation of orations and music. In 435 BC, he had the Odeon of Athens erected adjacent to the Theatre of Dionysius, and since the two structures were so near each other, the actors began to use the odeon as a place of rehearsal. In addition, the odeon actually had a roof, so spectators found it a convenient refuge if a sudden storm forced them out of the open theatre.

The roof of the Odeon of Athens has an interesting connection to history in two ways. First, when Aeschylus' play *The Persians* was first performed in 472 BC, part of the onstage scenery was created with the actual pavilion of Xerxes, seized by the victorious Greeks after the Battle of Plataea (479 BC). Plutarch reported that the pavilion figured also in the pyramid-like shape of the roof of Pericles' Odeon:

> The Odeum [Odeon], or music-room, which in its interior was full of seats and ranges of pillars, and outside had its roof made to slope and descend from one single point at the top, was constructed, we are told, in imitation of the King of Persia's Pavilion; this likewise by Pericles's order; which Cratinus again, in his comedy called *The Thracian Women*, made an occasion of raillery—
>
> > "So we see here,
> > Jupiter Long-pate Pericles appear,
> > Since ostracism time, he's laid aside his head,
> > And wears the new Odeum in its stead."[85]

It has even been argued that the pavilion itself stood atop the roof of the Odeon.[86]

Second, the Odeon was built as a replica of Xerxes' Hall of a Hundred Columns in Persepolis. Its dimensions (68.5 x 62.4 meters) were very near those of the Hall (68.5 x 68.5), and its columns were 9 x 10, very close to the size of the columns in the Hall (10 x 10).[87] Alas, though ruins of the Hall of a Hundred Columns survive to this day, the Odeon of Pericles was destroyed in the First Mithradatic War (87-86 BC).

Ruins of the Hall of a Hundred Columns in Persepolis

Demetrius and the Theatre of Dionysius

In 307 BC, the people in Athens were starving. Demetrius of Macedon had run a blockade against shipments of grain into the city, and conditions got so bad we are told that a father and a son fought over the right to win the honor of eating a dead mouse that had fallen from the ceiling. The Theatre of Dionysius figured almost immediately upon the arrival of Demetrius in Athens, as Plutarch recorded:

> In this condition was the city when Demetrius made his entrance and issued a proclamation that all the inhabitants should assemble in the theatre; which being done, he drew up his soldiers at the back of the stage, occupied the stage itself with his guards, and, presently coming in himself by the actor's passages, when the people's consternation had risen to its height, with his first words he put an end to it. Without any harshness of tone or bitterness of words, he reprehended them in a gentle and friendly way, and declared himself reconciled, adding a present of a hundred thousand bushels of wheat, and appointing as magistrates persons acceptable to the people. So Dromoclides the orator, seeing the people at a loss how to express their gratitude by any words or acclamations, and ready for anything that would outdo the verbal encomiums of the public speakers, came forward, and moved a decree for delivering Piræus and Munychia into the hands of king Demetrius.[88]

Demetrius I of Macedon with the horns of a bull, a symbol of Bacchus.

As time passed and Demetrius restored the freedoms suspended by the oligarchy, the politician Stratocles began to heap extravagant awards and honors on Demetrius, even elevating him to the status of a tutelary deity (their own special protective spirit) with the name *Soter* ("Preserver"). In fact, they actually "turned the feast of Bacchus, the Dionysia, into the Demetria, or feast of Demetrius"[89] and minted coins depict Demetrius with the horns of a bull, which was a symbol of Bacchus (see image).

Plutarch, however, is quick to note that the gods soon rebelled against all the extravagances of the Athenians, sending evils to show their disapproval. Where Dionysius (or Bacchus) was concerned, Plutarch says this about the poor Athenians::

They had to omit the solemn procession at the feast of Bacchus, as upon the very day of its celebration there was such a severe and rigorous frost, coming quite out of its time, that not only the vines and fig-trees were killed, but almost all the wheat was destroyed in the blade.[90]

One dramatist even saw a great opportunity for himself when Nature started to turn against Demetrius in this way. Says Plutarch:

Accordingly, Philippides, an enemy to Stratocles, attacked him in a comedy, in the following verses: —

> He for whom frosts that nipped your vines were sent,
> And for whose sins the holy robe was rent,
> Who grants to men the gods' own honors, he,
> Not the poor stage, is now the people's enemy.[91]

In summary, the narratives of Pericles and Demetrius show how the government and the theatre became entangled in ancient times.

THE ROMAN THEATRE

Chapter 9

Roman Innovations

During the Roman era, theatre structure continued along the lines established by the Greeks, but innovations were made. For example, the shape of the orchestra was changed from a circle to a semicircle. The skene expanded to the *scenae frons*, a two- or three-storey structure with as many as eighteen Corinthian columns and at least three doorways, which served as a permanent decorative background.

Roman theatre at Aphrodisias, Turkey, late first century BC. Note the lowered orchestra, which allowed for animal fights and water shows.

The Romans also elevated the stage (or *pulpitum*) to a height of about three feet to accommodate viewing. Under the stage, they placed pumping systems so that they could flood the orchestra for water shows.

As time passed, Roman architects began moving away from the need to situate theatres in mountainsides. Instead, in the mid first-century, they began using Roman concrete (*opus caementicium*) to erect structures on level ground, one example being the first theatre erected in Rome, the Theatre of Pompey.

The Theatre of Pompey in Rome

The Theatre of Pompey in Rome has a colorful history all its own. On one of his campaigns in the Mediterranean, the Roman general Pompey the Great, the staunch enemy of Julius Caesar, visited the city of Mitylene, where he attended the theatre to see the dramatic contests of the poets, "who took at that time no other theme or subject than the actions of Pompey." According to Plutarch, Pompey "was extremely pleased with the theatre itself, and had a model of it taken, intending to erect one in Rome on the same design, but larger and more magnificent."[92]

However, his idea was met with opposition in Rome from those Senators concerned about the relaxation of morals in the Republic at that time. To win them over, Pompey de-emphasized the theatre portion of his great architectural complex and billed it as a temple to Venus "under which we have placed tiers of seats for viewing the shows"[93]—he added, almost as an after-thought. His ploy worked, and the theatre opened in 55 BC.

Whether the great theatre brought glory to Pompey or not, it was impressive indeed as a Roman architectural accomplishment. It was over 147′ high and could hold 20,000 spectators. Extending eastward from the *scaena frons* was a huge portico lined with 100 columns and ornamented with lovely gardens that manifested the pleasures of civilization.

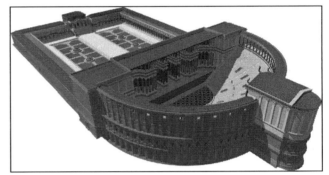

Model of the Theatre of Pompey with the Temple of Venus in the lower right corner and the curia in the upper left.

Displayed in the complex were the plundered treasures brought home by Pompey from the wars, and statuary abounded. The promised statue of Venus Victrix, Pompey's patron goddess, was erected on top of the cavea; statues personifying the conquered nations were raised; and a statue of Pompey himself, "fifteen hands high"[94] (37.5 feet), was erected as well (presumably smaller than the statue of Venus).

The great poets of the age may perhaps have noticed the irony of an event that took place at the foot of this statue on March 15, 44 BC. Four years earlier, Julius Caesar and Pompey had fallen out, and Pompey had fled to Egypt. There he fell victim to Ptolemy XIII, a young pharaoh who hoped to curry favor with Caesar by returning Pompey's head to Rome in a bag. Thus, Pompey's statue may have been deliberately chosen by the Senators as their point of their assault against Caesar, whom they assassinated on the steps to the curia in the theatre complex. Certainly William Shakespeare took note of the symbolism of this spot in his play *Julius Caesar*, where he penned these lines for Antony to speak in his great oration following the murder of Caesar:

> Then burst his mighty heart;
> And, in his mantle muffling up his face,
> Even at the base of Pompey's statue,
> Which all the while ran blood, great Caesar fell.[95]

Here the poet was referring to the superstitious belief of the ancients that a statue could bleed to express the emotions of the ghost of the departed—in this case, apparently the thrill of revenge.

Nor was the irony lost on the poet George Gordon, Lord Byron, who wrote in *Childe Harold's Pilgrimage*, even casting Pompey and Caesar as "puppets of a scene":

> And thou, dread statue! yet existent in
> The austerest form of naked majesty,
> Thou who beheldest, mid the assassins' din,
> At thy bathed base the bloody Caesar lie,
> Folding his robe in dying dignity,
> An offering to thine altar from the queen
> Of gods and men, great Nemesis! did he die,
> And thou, too, perish, Pompey? have ye been
> Victors of countless kings, or puppets of a scene?[96]

One last word about Pompey's statue: the statue on display at the Palazzo Spada (Spada Palace) in Rome was discovered buried in the theatre area in the seventeenth century. Though scholars disagree as to whether this is the statue connected to the assassination of Caesar, it nevertheless has a moment in theatre history all its own. Here are the words of the Irishman, Rev. John Chetwode Eustace, who reported on "the recent spoliations of the French" in 1813:

> While the French occupied Rome in the years 1798-99, etc., they erected in the centre of the Coliseum a temporary theatre where they acted various republican pieces for the amusement of the army and the improvement, I fancy, of such Romans as might be disposed to fraternize with them and adopt their principles. Voltaire's [play] *Brutus,* as may easily be imagined, was a favorite tragedy; and, in order to give it more effect, it was resolved to transport the very statue of Pompey, at the feet of which the dictator had fallen, to the

Coliseum, and erect it on the stage. The colossal size of the statue, and its extended arm, rendered it difficult to displace it; the arm was, therefore, sawed off for the conveyance and put on again at the Coliseum; and on the second removal of the statue, again taken off, and again replaced at the Palazzo de Spada. So friendly to Pompey was the republican enthusiasm of the French! So favorable to the arts and antiquities of Rome, their Love of Liberty![97]

The Ludi

Just as the Greek theatre was connected to the god Dionysius, the Roman theatre originated in festivals of thanksgiving to Jupiter, the chief god. Eventually other festivals were added in honor of Apollo, Ceres, and Cybele (the "Great Mother"), whose images would be borne as part of the festival parade. The word *ludi* derives from the Latin word for *games* because the earliest *ludi* were chariot races (called *ludi circenses*) and animal hunts (*venationes*), but at the end of the First Punic War (241 BC) officials beefed up the celebration by adding theatrical performances (*ludi scaenici*), with the nod going to the poet Livius Andronicus, whose works ushered in the Golden Age of Roman theater. From the earliest times, the *Ludi Romani* (Roman Games)

This detail of musicians from the Zliten mosaic (2nd century AD) was part of a scene of gladiatorial games and wild-animal events in the arena like those associated with the Roman ludi.

were held for three days in September. However, as the Roman Republic gave way to the Roman Empire, a fourth day was added for the worship of the emperor. This practice began two years after the assassination of Julius Caesar on January 1, 42 BC, the day he became the first emperor to be deified (declared to be a god). One can see how the association of plays with the worship of pagan gods—and even dead men—gave the *ludi* a certain stigma among early Christians, who, like the Jews, considered plays a form of idolatry.

The Golden Age of the Roman Theatre

During the First Punic War (264-261 BC), the Romans were brought into contact with Greek culture as they advanced into the region called Magna Graecia in southern Italy. No doubt, soldiers and generals became part of the audience at Greek plays and viewed them as a significant way in which the mantle of European leadership could pass from the fading Greek culture to the rising culture of the Romans. The greatest poet of the age—and the man deemed the "father of Roman literature"—Livius Andronicus began translating Greek plays into Latin so that they could be performed at the *ludi*. The honor of being the first person actually to compose plays in Latin, however, goes to Gnaeus Naevius (c. 270 – c. 201 BC). Naevius branched out from the Greek models and created a new genre of plays about Roman history and mythology—the *fabulae praetextae*, as they were called, after the *praetexta*, the purple-banded toga of the Roman nobles.

Mime had found its way to Rome by 211 BC, and Roman satire emerged with the poet Ennius (239-169 BC). Besides Ennius, the great poets of the Golden Age included Titus Maccius Plautus and the former slaves Caecilius Statius and Terence. The Golden Age of drama ended in 140 BC when the Roman blood thirst drew spectators away from theatres and to the gladiatorial games in the Forum. When freedom of speech disappeared in the period of the Early Roman Empire, few poets chose to compose plays, and except for Seneca, who is generally listed among the poets of the Silver Age of Roman literature.

Forms of Roman "Entertainment"

In a way, it is hard to describe the change of direction of the Roman theatre as a "development" of theatre, in general. It is perhaps better described as a "degeneration," though certainly the Greeks had some disgusting presentations, as Aristotle pointed out in his *Poetics*. But Greece saw nothing like what developed in the Roman period, especially during the Empire.

The story begins nicely enough in 364 BC when the Etruscans put on festivals involving music and dance, but the degraded aspect of Roman entertainment began with what are called the Attelan plays, so named because they originated in a place called Atella, which is about 113 miles southwest of Rome, as the crow flies. The Attelan plays are classified as *low farces,* which means they used vulgar language, rude jokes, and what the rich people saw as the buffoonish nature of the poor. (If you've ever seen a *Punch and Judy* show, you've probably gotten a taste of a low farce.) According to Tacitus, they became "so horrid" that they had to be banished from Rome in 28 AD.

The Amphitheatres

At first, the Romans built theatres on the Greek model, but as their lust for spectacles such as animal fights and gladiatorial games developed, the theatre changed to accommodate the purpose. Excavations at the ruins of the great Roman theatre at Apamea Syria, for example, have shown how terra cotta water systems were built to channel water down into the orchestra area so that *naumachiae* (naval battles) could be re-enacted in the theatres.

The Greek theatre was semicircular in shape, but the Roman amphitheatre was circular. This is a little easier to understand if one knows that the prefix *amphi-* means *both,* so an amphitheatre is a theatre that has seating on "both sides."

A theatre with a circular orchestra and semi-circular seating.

An amphitheatre (the Roman Coliseum), circular in shape with an oval-shaped performance area and seating all around.

In our times, the content of plays, TV shows, and movies is influenced, to a certain degree, by what the public is willing to pay for. Producers are more likely to turn a profit if they can attract a lot of paying customers. However, this is not the way things worked in ancient Rome. Because the emperors often worried about uprisings from people who did not have enough to eat, they adopted a policy of giving them grain and entertainment to keep them pacified. In 100 AD, the satirist Juvenal expressed his disgust with the downward path of the Roman populace:

> *Nam qui dabat olim imperium fasces legiones omnia, nunc se continet atque duas tantum res anxius optat, panem et circenses.*

> The people that once bestowed commands, consulships, legions and all else, now meddles no more and longs eagerly for just two things—Bread and Games!"[98]

The Theatre of Marcus Scaurus

In his *Natural History*, Pliny the Elder (23-79 AD) described the amazing architectural "extravagance" of Marcus Scaurus, who held the office of aedile in 58 BC. It was the office of the aedile to maintain public buildings and regulate public festivals, and Scaurus was not a man to skimp. It probably did not hurt that Roman generals, including Scaurus' stepfather Sulla, were hauling Greek statues and columns back to Rome by the thousands, so many that it is said there were more statues than inhabitants in the city. Pliny, who disapproved of the excess, left us this description of the fate of some of its properties:

> As aedile Scaurus built the greatest building that was ever constructed by man. It was greater not only than any temporary works but also those that had been planned to last for ever. This was a theatre that had a three-tiered stage with 360 columns—in a city that previously had not tolerated 6 columns of Hymettan marble without criticizing a distinguished citizen. The lowest tier of the stage was of marble, the middle one of glass—an unheard of example of extravagance even in later times—and the top one of gilded planks. The columns of the lowest tier were each almost 38 feet high.

> The bronze statues in the spaces between the columns were 3,000 in number. The auditorium held 80,000—yet Pompey's theatre seating 40,000 is

sufficiently large now, even though the city is many times larger and the population much more numerous. The rest of the theatre's equipment—including costumes interwoven with gold thread, scenery, and other properties—was on such a scale that when surplus items of everyday use were taken to Scaurus' villa at Tusculum and the house itself was set ablaze and burnt down by angry servants, he lost 30 million sesterces.

Scaurus gained one advantage from that fire: no one could emulate his madness in the future.[99]

The Theatre of Curio the Younger

Though it would be hard to top the "eye candy" of Scaurus' theatre, the prize for mechanical genius in the Roman theatre would probably go to the engineers who constructed the theatre of Curio the Younger, who was aedile in 50 AD. Again, Pliny provides the description and commentary on this marvel:

> Curio built two vast wooden theatres side by side, each balanced on a revolving pivot. Before midday, a performance of a play was staged in both; the theatres faced in opposite directions so that the actors should not drown each other's lines. Then suddenly the theatres revolved (it is agreed that after the first few days this happened while some of the audience actually remained in their seats), and their corners came together to become an amphitheatre. Here Curio staged fights between gladiators—although the Roman people found themselves in even greater danger than the gladiators, as Curio spun them around.

> It is difficult to know what should amaze us more, the inventor or the invention, or the sheer audacity of the conception. Most amazing of all is the madness of a people rash enough to sit in such treacherous and unstable seats!

> What contempt for human life this shows! How can we justify our complaints about Cannae! What a disaster this could have been! Here the whole Roman people, as if put on board two ships, were supported by a pair of pivots and watched themselves fighting for their lives and likely to perish at any moment should the mechanism be put out of gear![100]

Horace's Rules for Drama

In 19 BC, the Roman poet Horace wrote a letter to his friend Piso, the Roman senator and consul, in which he set out the basic principles of poetry. This epistle, which has come to be called the *Ars Poetica (Poetic Art)*, gave a nod to the principles of Greek drama outlined by Aristotle and added a few innovations.

Statue of Horace in Venosa, Italy

Subject Matter

Horace recommended that Romans could "either follow tradition or invent a consistent story." Traditional characters, such as Achilles, Medea, and Orestes, were to remain as they had been in Greek literature, and new characters were to be handled "with a consistency of their own." He especially recommended the themes of Homer, where the characters had "well-known traits" and did not think it advisable to "attempt something distinctly original." Not to be completely discouraging of creativity, however, Horace added that even with such famous stories a Roman could make a name for himself if he handled his material "in an original fashion." Was this what Seneca was thinking when he out-goried the Greeks in his portrayal of Medea?

Representing Life and Action

Horace advised the Romans to "study the 'strange, eventful history' of human life, and note the characteristics of the several ages of man, so that the different periods may not be confused." Perhaps this principle underlies the development of *stock characters* in Roman plays, that is, character types that authors used again and again. Among these were the *adulescens* (the young, rich, love-struck hero) and the *senex* (the old man whom the *adulescens* may fear, but not respect).

Whereas the "action" in a Greek play often took place offstage and was simply reported by a messenger, Horace allowed that events could be actually presented on the stage. However, like the Greeks, he felt that narrative would be best "in the case of revolting and incredible incidents."

Actors and Chorus

Horace cautioned against having more than three characters on the stage at one time. He retained the Chorus but felt it "should take a real part in the action." The Chorus was not to sing anything that was not necessary for the play, and it should always "promote the cause of morality and religion."

Plot

Horace introduced the plot that extended over five acts. Like Aristotle, he discouraged the use of the *deus ex machina*, which both apparently viewed as an uncreative way to resolve a character's dilemma.

Diction

Like Aristotle, Horace urged dramatists to be careful in their choice of language but did allow that, even when using the old stories of the Greeks, they could give "a fresh tone" to a familiar story with "the skillful combination" of words.

He also followed Aristotle's suggestion that a writer coin a few words of his own "in moderation as the old poets used to do." The playwright Plautus (254-184 BC) is particularly famous for this. For example, he coined the word *dentifrangibula* ("tooth-crackers") to refer to fists in *Bacchides* and *oculicrepidae* ("clatter-eyed") in *Trinummus*. Another comic writer, named Laberius (105-43 BC), coined the verb *adulescenturire* ("to behave like a youth") to describe the behavior of someone who was not acting his age.

Tone

Horace believed that Tragedy and Comedy were too different in tone to be presented in the same play. Recognizing the emotional power of a play, he said, "Above all things, a play must appeal to the feelings of an audience, and the language must be adapted to the characters impersonated. Where there is lack of such agreement, everybody will laugh in scorn." In short, a hero should speak like a hero, and a goatherd like a goatherd.

The Emergence of Spectacle and Cruelty

Greek plays may have handled adult themes and naughty language, but what came next among the Romans outdid the Greeks by far. Whereas Aristotle had placed the element of Spectacle at the bottom of his list of theatrical components, the Romans set Aristotle on his head and placed Spectacle as the end-all and be-all of entertainment. This was, of course, due in part to the efforts of the emperors to keep the masses entertained, and therefore passive. After all, who will get up a conspiracy against the government when he can more easily spend a day at the theatres or amphitheatres and experience the thrills of lust and murder—and not always just "acted"?

Gladiators and *Bestiarii*

When we think of the Roman amphitheatres, we think first and foremost of the gladiatorial shows—spectacles in which men, mostly slaves and prisoners of war, would fight to the death before crowds ranging from 20,000 to 50,000, depending on the location. Some of them became famous and are known to us by name—especially those involved in the gladiatorial revolts: Spartacus, Crixus, and Oenamaus.

Roman mosaic depicting *bestiarii*. Note the man being attacked by a leopard in the upper left quarter.

But the theatres and amphitheatres were used also for savage animal fights, or *bestiarii*, with excesses that, as people charged with the stewardship of God's creatures, we can hardly imagine today. In AD 80, at the games of the Emperor Titus, 9,000 animals (both wild and tame) were slaughtered over a period of 100 days for the amusement of the spectators. In 107, the Emperor Trajan, not to be outdone, oversaw the slaughter of 11,000 animals in shows lasting for 120 days as he celebrated his victory over the Dacians.

Not only were land animals such as lions, bears, and bulls used in these spectacles, but aquatic animals as well, which was made possible by the Roman engineers who found a way to channel water into the amphitheatre to flood the orchestra. Pliny the Elder noted that Marcus Scaurus was the first to display in his marvelous theatre "one hippopotamus and four crocodiles, swimming in a temporary pool."[101] Dio Cassius noted that on one occasion in the reign of Augustus the circus was flooded not just for an aquatic exhibit, but for the slaughter of thirty-six crocodiles.[102]

Naumachiae (Mock Naval Battles)

The flooding of the amphitheatres also facilitated *naumachiae*, re-enactments of naval battles for the thrill of the crowd. This boast about Titus's grandiose *naumachiae* appears in the *Epigrams* of Martial:

Depiction of a *naumachia* by Giovanni Lanfranco, painted 1635-38

The task of Augustus had been to embattle fleets, and to arouse the waves with the sound of the naval trumpet. How inferior is this to what our Caesar accomplishes! Thetis and Galatea have beheld in the waves wild animals previously unknown to them, Triton has seen chariots glowing along the foaming ocean course, and thought the steeds of his master were passing before him; and Nereus, while he was preparing fierce contests with bold vessels, shrunk from going on foot through the liquid ways. Whatever is seen in the circus and the amphitheatre, the rich lake of Caesar has shown to thee. Let Fucinus, and the ponds of the dire Nero, be vaunted no more; and let ages to come remember but this one sea-fight.[103]

Dio recorded that these sea battles, like the gladiator contests, were fought to the death with the ranks of the "actors" being supplied by prisoners of war and condemned criminals.[104]

Executions

Such slaughter was not simply the province of the great spectacles in the amphitheatres. Actual killings took place during the performance of plays as well. Martial described how a condemned criminal named Laureolus was crucified and torn to death by a bear as part of a performance:

> As first, bound down upon the Scythian rock, Prometheus with ever-renewed vitals feasted the untiring vulture, so has Laureolus, suspended on no feigned cross, offered his defenceless entrails to a Caledonian bear. His mangled limbs quivered, every part dripping with gore, and in his whole body no shape was to be found. In short, he suffered such punishment as one who had been guilty of parricide, or who had cut his master's throat, or had insanely despoiled the temples of their hidden gold, or had applied the incendiary torch to thee, O Rome. This criminal had surpassed the crimes of ancient story, and what had been fabulous, was in his case *a real punishment.*[105]

Martial also narrated the manner in which a condemned criminal was once costumed as the mythological Orpheus and actually put to death in the presentation of the myth.

> Whatever Rhodope is said to have beheld upon Orpheus' stage, your arena, Caesar, has exhibited to you. Rocks have crept along, and, marvelous sight! a wood, such as the grove of the Hesperides is believed to have been, has run. There was to be seen every species of wild beast mingled with flocks, and above the poet hung many a bird. But he himself was laid low, torn by an ungrateful bear. *Thus, however, this story, which was before but a fiction, has now become fact* (emphasis added).[106]

The geographer Strabo was an eyewitness to the execution of a rebel who was executed in a manner that required the construction of special apparatus:

> And recently, in my own time, a certain Selurus, called the "son of Aetna," was sent up to Rome because he had put himself at the head of an army and for a

long time had overrun the regions round about Aetna with frequent raids; I saw him torn to pieces by wild beasts at an appointed combat of gladiators in the Forum; for he was placed on a lofty scaffold, as though on Aetna, and the scaffold was made suddenly to break up and collapse, and he himself was carried down with it into cages of wild-beasts — fragile cages that had been prepared beneath the scaffold for that purpose.[107]

In AD 197, the Christian writer Tertullian wrote an invective against pagan religious tales in which, during re-enactments, "the poor actors were forced to suffer to the life and be the very gods themselves."[108] To prove his point, he told how a man (perhaps a criminal or a condemned Christian), apparently substituted at the right moment for the actor playing the role of Hercules, was deliberately burnt to death in the telling of the tale. Tertullian also recorded how Christian women were tied to the horns of a bull and dragged through the arena until dead, in imitation of the myth of Dirce.

Mimes

Today the word *mime* calls up the image of Bip the Clown, the character created by the French actor, Marcel Marceau (1923-2007)—a clown in white-face and wearing white gloves—who acted out a story employing only gesture, facial expression, and body movement. Marceau referred to his art as "the art of silence," and certainly it is considered a genuine art form which can help us understand the human condition. However, that is not what the word *mime* meant in the context of the Roman Empire.

Marcel Marceau as Bip the Clown

To understand the nature of the Roman mime, one must understand its origins in the Atellan farces. These were low comedies of a vulgar, buffoonish nature which originated in the town of Atella and were introduced into Rome as early as 391 BC. (They are sometimes referred to as Oscan farces because of the language in which they originated.)

The garb of the mime, at least in the early period, has been compared to that of a harlequin. That is, they wore a patchwork coat of many colors called a *centunculus*. They also used soot to blacken their faces, shaved their heads, and went barefoot.

As Roman taste degenerated and the degraded spectacle became popular, the Romans moved away from traditional tragedy and comedy and began to go in for the mime, which really was not much more than a skit—and a crude one at that. In the later Empire, mimes were more like the X-rated movie in our own time. Even a pagan Roman like Ovid, who did not shy away from adult themes in his own poetry, reviled the graphic nature and language of the mime as *obscena* [obscene] and *turpia* [disgraceful].[109]

One novelty introduced by the mimes was the appearance of actresses on the stage, and though actresses today might view this development in a positive light, one must keep in mind that in the Roman Empire, as a matter of law, actresses were at the bottom of the social scale, ranked in the same class as prostitutes. In fact, since the theme of the mimes was invariably adultery and since the eighteen-year-old Emperor Elagabalus had demanded realistic portrayal on the stage, some considered the terms *actress* and *prostitute* to be synonyms. After all, it was thought, an actress, like a prostitute, was selling herself in a "desire to seduce the audience."[110]

In addition to the presence of scantily-clad women in adulterous skits, the mimes occasionally slipped into political insult. In his *Annals*, Tacitus made a record of this tendency in the section that covers the years AD 14-15:

> Meanwhile the unruly tone of the theatre which first showed itself in the preceding year, broke out with worse violence, and some soldiers and a centurion, besides several of the populace, were killed, and the tribune of a praetorian cohort was wounded, while they were trying to stop insults to the magistrates and the strife of the mob.[111]

Various measures were undertaken to bring the actors under control (though, by a law of Augustus, they could not be scourged), but these did not bring an end to the problem. Complaints of the degraded subject matter and lewd behavior of the mimes also continued, and finally the Emperor Tiberius had to act: Tacitus records the following for the year AD 28:

> Next, after various and usually fruitless complaints from the praetors, the emperor finally brought forward a motion about the licentious behaviour of the players. "They had often," he said, "sought to disturb the public peace, and to

bring disgrace on private families, and the old Oscan farce, once a wretched amusement for the vulgar, had become at once so indecent and so popular, that it must be checked by the Senate's authority." The players, upon this, were banished from Italy.[112]

"Wretched," "vulgar," and "indecent"—these are the descriptions of the pagan Romans themselves, and we should not be surprised that the early Christians were similarly put off, as we will see anon.

Objections to the Theatre among Non-Christians

Just as Plato (and Aristotle, to a degree) had insight into the dangerous influence of the theatre, so Roman commentators showed concerns of their own. First under consideration will be the concerns of those who were not influenced by the teaching of Hebrew Scripture, that is to say, the pagan and secular Romans.

Ovid

In AD 8, the poet Ovid was banished from Rome by the Emperor Augustus, but, protesting what he perceived as an unjust act, he wrote a series of letters to the emperor which have been collected under the title *Tristia*, or *Lamentations*. Examine them to see what light they shed on the practices of the Roman mimes.

Ovid (43 BC – c. AD 18)

Excerpt from "The Poet's Plea"
By Ovid

What if I had written foul-jesting mimes which always contain the sin of forbidden love, in which constantly a well-dressed adulterer appears and the artful wife fools her stupid husband? These are viewed by the marriageable maiden, the wife, the husband, and the child; even the senate in large part is present. Nor is it enough that the ear is outraged with impure words; the eyes grow accustomed to many shameful sights, and when the lover has deceived the husband by some novel trick, there is applause and he is presented amid great favour with the palm. Because the stage is not moral, it is profitable to the poet, and these great immoralities are bought at no small price by the praetor. Run over the expenses of thine own games, Augustus, and thou wilt read of many things of this sort that cost thee dear. These thou has thyself viewed and oft presented to the view of others so benign is thy majesty everywhere, and with thine eyes, by which the whole world profits, thou hast gazed undisturbed at these adulteries of the stage. If 'tis right to compose mimes that copy vice, to my themes a smaller penalty is due. Can it be that this type of writing is rendered safe by the stage to which it belongs that the license of the mimes has been granted by the theatre?[113]

EXERCISE 9.1: Analyzing a Primary Source (Ovid)

Direction: Use the letter of Ovid to draw out insights into what went on in the Roman mimes by answering the questions below.

1. In the opening sentence, what adjective does Ovid use to describe the "jesting" mimes?

2. What kind of "love" does he accuse the mimes of presenting?

3. According to Ovid, what was the typical audience reaction to the deceitful wives presented in the mimes?

4. In Ovid's opinion, what made the plays so financially profitable?

5. What difference does Ovid draw between his own works and those of the mimes?

Pliny the Younger

Pliny the Younger (AD 61- c. 113) gives us a peek into attitudes toward the Roman mimes when he describes the practice of a nearly eighty-year-old woman named Ummidia Quadratillia regarding her grandson Quadratus, which appears below.

Excerpt from "Letter to Geminus" By Pliny the Younger

He [Quadratus] lived in the family of his grandmother, who was exceedingly devoted to the pleasures of the town, with great severity of conduct, yet at the same time with the utmost compliance. She retained a set of pantomimes, whom she encouraged more than becomes a lady of quality. But Quadratus never witnessed their performances, either when she exhibited them in the theatre, or in her own house; nor did she exact his attendance. I once heard her say, when she was commending her grandson's oratorical studies to my care, that it was her habit, being a woman and as such debarred from active life, to amuse herself with playing at chess or backgammon, and to look on at the mimicry of her pantomimes; but that before engaging in either diversion, she constantly sent away her grandson to his studies: a custom, I imagine, which she observed as much out of a certain reverence, as affection, to the youth.[114]

EXERCISE 9.2: Analyzing a Primary Source (Pliny the Younger)

<u>Directions</u>: What can we learn about the Roman mimes by reading the letter of Pliny the Younger to his friend Geminus? The questions below will help you extract some insights.

1. What does the second sentence reveal to you about Pliny's attitude toward Ummidia Quadratillia's support of the pantomimes?

2. We learn from Pliny that the mimes were not only performed in the theatres, but

   in _____

3. What excuse did Ummidia Quadratillia give to Pliny for her choice of amusement?

4. Construct a syllogism that shows the reasoning underlying Ummidia's excuse. Then test it for soundness.

   Major premise:

   Minor premise:

   Conclusion:

   Your observations:_____

5. What was Ummidia's position regarding her grandson and the mimes?

6. What does Ummidia's position reveal to you about the content of the mimes?

Early Christian Responses to the Roman Theatre

The picture that emerges of the Roman theatres and amphitheatres in the Roman Empire is not a pretty one. Actual killings taking place on stage, adultery, vulgarity, nudity, fistfights—these are the behaviors associated with the word *theatre* at the time of the Early Church. On top of that, there were the spectacles in the amphitheatre where criminals and prisoners of war would be executed in gladiator "contests" and where Christians—men, women, and children—would be torn apart by wild beasts to the cheers of the crowd. If any group of Christians was ever in a position to ask, "WWJD?"[5] it was these early believers.

But it was not simply the ugliness of the shows themselves that faced the Christians. There was the matter of the legal status and social standing of the actors and actresses themselves. How were Christians to treat these people, knowing they were children of God, equal to themselves in His eyes, and simply sinners for whom Christ had died, like the rest of them?

The fact is that, unlike today when a porn star might turn her life over to Christ and move forward on a better path, actresses and actors in the Roman Empire had a legal status that kept them bound to the theatres. Not only were actresses classed by law in the same group as prostitutes, there were marriage restrictions that kept them from rising in society. Specifically, they—and their children—were prohibited by law from marrying a Senator. Nor could they marry a Senator's son, grandson, or great-grandson, and so strong was the prejudice against them that they were considered naturally (genetically) inferior people who passed their inferiority to their children.

What is more, because of laws governing slavery in the Empire, actors and actresses were not allowed to leave their profession. As one historian has explained it:

> In addition to slaves there were women of the lower class *"ex viliori sorte progenitae"* who were obligated to the compulsory performance of the spectacles *"spectaculorum debentur obsequiis"*. . . . Similarly the daughter of theatrical parents who appeared to be living a vulgar life *(vulgarem vitam)* was obligated to appear on stage. . . .[115]

What, then, was the Christian community to do when an actor or actress converted to Christ? First, as with all believers, actors and actresses were to leave the stage before they received baptism, which the Church believed was in keeping with Scripture:

> Therefore go out from their midst,
> and be separate from them, says the Lord,
> and touch no unclean thing;
> then I will welcome you,
> and I will be a father to you,

---

[5] What Would Jesus Do? (a catch-phrase employed by young Christians in the twenty-first century)

> and you shall be sons and daughters to me,
> says the Lord Almighty" (2 Cor. 6:17-18).

However, though God had promised to give them a clean slate, the state had not their legal bondage to the stage meant that a death-bed conversion was really their only guarantee of freedom in this regard. Christians were powerless to effect any change until the time when the emperors themselves were Christian.

In AD 380, Christian Emperor Theodosius ruled that women who had been baptized would not be forced to return to the stage:

Early Christian depiction of preparation for baptism

> "For we forbid women to be returned to this duty, if a better mode of living has released them from the ties of their natural condition. We also order that such women remain free from the ignoble mark of any prejudice derived from the stage, if they have obtained exemption from this compulsory public service of a coarse character by a special grant of Imperial favor of our Clemency.[116]

Freedom from compulsory service and freedom from social stigma—Christians set free in this manner could hardly have asked for more.

Besides the common theme of adultery, the mimes were offensive to the early Christians in another, perhaps more direct way as well: They often mocked the crucifixion of Christ. According to Professor Charlambos Bakirtzis, a Greek archaeologist, some surviving third-century graffiti has left us with a rendering of the particulars of these skits. The image he describes shows a worshipper gazing up at "a crucified mime

The Alexamanos graffitio

wearing hose, singlet, and a donkey mask" alongside the words "Alexamanos worships God."[117] Such a depiction would, of course, have been a sacrilege to any believer.

Yet, horrible as they were, these mimes sometimes had an unexpected result. Sometimes these pagan actors underwent an actual spiritual transformation during the performance. During the reign of Emperor Maximian Galerius (305-311), for example, a well-known actor named Ardalion was playing the role of a Christian who renounced Christ after first refusing to sacrifice to idols. However, during the performance, Ardalion stepped forward, asked the spectators to stop jeering, and announced that he was, in fact, a Christian. Refusing to recant, he was burned to death on a blazing-hot iron grill.[118]

Another example is that of Porphyrios, a popular mime who was invited to perform at the birthday celebration of Julian the Apostate, an emperor born to a Christian family who had renounced the faith. On November 4, AD 361, Porphyrios and the actors playing the Christian clergy appeared onstage costumed as a priest, a bishop, and the convert, deriding the ritual in a manner designed to get a laugh from the emperor. During the pretended ritual, Porphyrios sarcastically delivered the line, "The Servant of the Lord Jesus Christ, Porphyrios is baptized in the name of the Father and the Son and the Holy Spirit." However, in the next scene, when the script called for him to be dressed into the garb of a newly baptized Christian, a change came over him, and he declared from the stage that he had, during the baptism scene, actually accepted Christ. Refusing like Ardalion to recant, Porphyrios was beheaded.[119]

Considering all that went on in the theatres of Rome in this period, it is hardly surprising that the Early Church Fathers were hostile to the theatre. In this respect, their voices joined the invectives of the pagan authors Ovid and Pliny the Younger.

EXERCISE 9.3: Analyzing a Primary Source (Chrysostom)

Directions: Please read the excerpt below about the immorality of the Roman stage plays. It was written by John of Chrysostom [krĭ-SŎS-təm] (AD c. 349-407), the archbishop of Constantinople and one of the Early Church Fathers. Chrysostom was a witness to the excesses of the late Roman Empire as well as to the terror of the barbarian invasions. After reading the excerpt, please answer the questions that follow.

Excerpt from "Homily 37: Matthew 11:7-9"
By John of Chrysostom

After reviling the vulgar speech and the coarse laughter offered up for the often disgusting scenes of some plays, Chrysostom wrote this:

[1] For even all the mire that is there poured out for you, by the speeches, by the songs, by the laughter, ye collect and take every man to his home, or rather not to his home only, but every man even into his own mind.

[2] And from things not worthy of abhorrence thou turnest away; while others which are to be abhorred, so far from hating, thou doest even court. Many, for instance, on coming back from tombs, are used to wash[ing] themselves, but on returning from theatres they have never groaned, nor poured forth any fountains of tears. Yet surely the dead man is no unclean thing, whereas sin induces such a blot, that not even with ten thousand fountains could one purge it away, but with tears only, and with confessions. . . .

[3] And what again is the applause? What the tumult, and the satanical cries, and the devilish gestures? For first one, being a young man, wears his hair long behind, and changing his nature into that of a woman, is striving both in aspect, and in gesture, and in garments, and generally in all ways, to pass into the likeness of a tender damsel. . . . [I]ndeed both adulteries and stolen marriages are there, and there are women playing the harlot, men prostituting, youths corrupting themselves: all there is iniquity to the full, all sorcery, all shame. Wherefore they that sit by should not laugh at these things, but weep and groan bitterly. . . .

[4] "What then? Are we to shut up the stage?" it will be said. "And are all things to be turned upside down at thy word?" Nay, but as it is, all things are turned upside down. . . ."Let us then pull down the stage," say they. Would that it were possible to pull it down. . . . Nevertheless, I enjoin no such thing. Standing as these places are, I bid you make them of no effect; which thing were a greater praise than pulling them down. . . .

[5] Thou hast a wife, thou hast children. What is equal to this pleasure? . . . To this purpose, we are told, that the Barbarians uttered on some occasion a saying

full of wise severity. I mean, that having heard of these wicked spectacles, and the unseasonable delight of them, "Why, the Romans," say they, "have devised these pleasures, as though they had not wives and children," implying that nothing is sweeter than children and wife, if thou are willing to live honestly.[120]

1. In Paragraph 1, Chrysostom laments the fact that theatre-goers bring the mire of

the stage not only into their homes, but, worse, into their_____

2. In Paragraph 2, Chrysostom compares men who return from the tombs and men who return from the theatres. What point is he trying to make in this comparison?

3. a. In the first part of Paragraph 3, what kind of stage portrayal is Chrysostom decrying?

   b. In the second part of Paragraph 3, what stage portrayals does he condemn?

4. In Paragraph 4, does Chrysostom say the theatres should be closed or torn down? In your own words, explain what he considers the best response of the Christian community to the theatre of his time.

5. a. In Paragraph 5, what group (besides the Christians) were shocked at the adultery displayed on the Roman stage?

b. Why do you suppose Chrysostom, who was writing for a Christian audience, included this information?

Augustine of Hippo

Augustine of Hippo (AD 354-430) was born in Roman North Africa in Thaghaste (now in Algeria). His father, a Roman official, was a pagan until his conversion to Christ on his deathbed, but his mother, Monica, was a devout Christian who constantly prayed for her son to know Christ.   Today Augustine is known as one of the great Fathers of the Church, but there was a time when Monica nearly despaired of her son's salvation. After his conversion (which is an interesting story in and of itself), Augustine reflected on his former willingness to go along unquestioningly with Roman culture saying, in part, " I was much attracted by the theatre, because the plays reflected my own unhappy plight and were tinder to my fire."[121] However, in his work *The City of God*, Augustine approached the subject from a theological, rather than a personal point of view. The excerpt below immediately follows his review of Plato's comments about the negative influence of the tales of the misbehaving gods.

Augustine and his mother Monica painted by Ary Sheffer, 1846

EXERCISE 9.4: Analyzing a Primary Source (Augustine)

<u>Directions</u>: Please read the excerpt from Augustine's *City of God* and answer the questions that follow.

Excerpt from *The City of God*
By Augustine of Hippo

But, some one will interpose, these [tales about the adulteries of the gods] are fables of poets, not the deliverances of gods themselves. Well, I have no mind to arbitrate between the lewdness of entertainments and of mystic rites; only I say, and history bears me out in making the assertion, that those same entertainments, in which the fictions of poets are the main attraction, were not introduced in festivals of the gods by the ignorant devotion of Romans, but that the gods themselves gave the most urgent commands to this effect, indeed extorted from the Romans these solemnities and celebrations in their honor. I touched on this in the preceding book, and mentioned that dramatic entertainments were first inaugurated at Rome on occasion of pestilence, and by authority of the pontiff [high priest]. And what man is there who is not more likely to adopt, for the regulation of his own life, the examples that are represented in plays which have a divine sanction, rather than the precepts written and promulgated with no more than human authority? If the poets gave false representation of Jove in describing him as adulterous, then it were to be expected the chaste gods should in anger avenge so wicked a fiction, in place of encouraging the games which circulated it. Of these plays, the most inoffensive are comedies and tragedies, that is to say, the dramas which poets write for the stage, and which, though they often handle impure subjects, yet do so without the filthiness of language which characterizes many other performances; and it is these dramas which boys are obliged by their seniors to read and learn as a part of what is called a liberal and gentlemanly education.[122]

Questions:

1. From Augustine's point of view, the theatrical plays were not founded by_____

_____, but by _____

2. Knowing his foundational belief about this issue, construct the syllogism that underlies the argument he makes in this passage.

Major premise: _____

Minor premise:_____

Conclusion:_____

Your observations: _____

3. In the last six lines of the passage (beginning "Of these plays . . . ."), Augustine seems to divide the classical dramas into two groups.

    a. What are the two groups?

    b. What seems to be his attitude toward the second group? Why?

ROMAN PLAYERS AND PLAYWRIGHTS

Chapter 10

Roscius the Comedian

The story of Roscius begins with a snake. In Lanuvium, where Roscius was born into slavery in 136 BC, snakes were esteemed as the incarnation of the goddess Juno Sospita. Therefore, families liked to keep a garden snake or two in the home in order to bring good fortune, so it was taken as a good omen when the baby Roscius was visited by one of these serpents. Cicero later told the story, thus:

> It is said that during [Roscius'] infancy his nurse awoke one night and was aghast at perceiving by the dim light of the night lamp that a serpent had crept into the cradle and was coiled round the sleeping infant. She screamed aloud at the sight, but his father related the event to the oracle, who predicted that the child would surpass all others in fame and glory. . . .[123]

The slave owner may well have recalled the cradle omen as Roscius grew and began to show not only the graceful movement required of a good actor, but also an impressive sense for mimicry. Perhaps, like the class clown of today, young Roscius regaled his friends with laughter by mimicking community members with easily identifiable quirks. Whatever it was that brought his abilities to his master's attention, the man would have known that, according to the law of the time, a slave's earnings were paid all or in part to the master. Therefore, with a view toward a career in the theatre for his slave, the

Denarius serratus of 64 BC depicting the cult of Juno Sospita

master arranged for Roscius to receive acting lessons, an opportunity which the budding actor did not let go to waste, eventually saving enough money to earn his freedom.

Though no paintings or sculptures of Roscius exist, the Roman consul Quintus Lutatius Catulus left this stunning appraisal:

Constiteram exorientem Auroram forte salutans,
cum subito a laeva Roscius exoritur.
Pace mihi liceat, caelestes, dicere vestra:
mortalis visus pulchrior esse deo.

I stood and to the Dawn my vows address'd
When Roscius rose refulgent in the west.
 Forgive, ye Powers! A mortal seem'd more bright
Than the bright god who darts the shafts of light.[124]

Such praise is all the more surprising when one reads that Roscius had "a pronounced squint" and was "cross-eyed" from birth.[125]

Roscius never let "well enough" alone. He could not tolerate any fault in himself, and he would practice in front of a mirror to perfect his skill. With a fellow actor named Aesopus, he would hang out in the Forum just to observe the orator Hortensius, who was famous for his gesticulations. Such a close observer of others he became that Julius Caesar once said, "I am often astonished at the impudence of those who act upon the stage while Roscius is a spectator of their attitudes; for who can make the least motion without Roscius seeing his imperfections?"[126]

How did the theatre-goers of Rome respond to Roscius? Well, we get a hint from Cicero, who wished that, upon the arrival of any good orator, "profound silence should ensue which is so significant a sign of awe and admiration that tears or laughter should break out at his pleasure; in short, that if anyone could observe the faces of the assembly, they would be led to believe that Roscius was speaking."[127] High praise, indeed!

Having achieved fame on the stage, Roscius eventually began to receive students. He demanded no less from them than from himself. As Cicero recorded, "I hear Roscius declaring that so far he has never succeeded in finding a single pupil of whom he really approved; not that there were not some who were acceptable, but because, if there was any blemish whatever in them, he himself could not endure it."[128]

The most famous of his students was the acclaimed orator Cicero himself, who reported that Roscius also took in a failing actor named Panurgus, who began to achieve fame once it was simply known that Roscius was his teacher! And Eros, who had been hissed off the stage, so poor were his skills, fled to Roscius' house for protection and instruction—and his star, too, began to rise.

In addition to appreciating his acting and teaching, the Roman literary public was happy to include Roscius, the one-time slave boy with snakes entwining his crib, as the writer of a book, in which he compared oratory and acting, and one scholar has even suggested that he may have had a hand in composing Cicero's famous work *On Oratory*.[129]

Though often identified as "Roscius the comedian," Cicero once described the masterful way Roscius delivered the line, "Father! My country! House of Priam!"—lines which suggest a role in a tragedy.[130]

Sulla, the Roman general and statesman, honored Roscius by making him an *eques Romani* (Roman knight) and even presented him the *anulus aureus,* the gold ring reserved for senators and magistrates. As time passed, the aging actor, unable to move as deftly as he had as a youth, adapted by asking the flute players to adjust their measures to his slowing pace. Ultimately, death found him in 62 BC.

Seneca

At about the same time that Jesus of Nazareth was being born in the Roman province of Palestine, Lucius Annaeus Seneca was being born in the province of Hispania. That places him among the first Gentiles to hear the gospel message, and since he was a philosopher and dramatist, one wonders what thought he gave to the message of the Christians in Rome, especially Paul. As it turns out, some research has gone into this subject over the years.

Lucius Annaeus Seneca
"Seneca the Younger"
(4 BC – AD 65)

Early Years

Seneca was born in the provincial capital, Corduba. When he was four or five years old, his aunt (his mother's sister) decided to take him to Rome, where his father had made a name for himself as a rhetoric teacher. It was a trip of about 1,500 miles, on foot. They would have headed eastward and northward on the Via Augusta until they hooked up with the Via Domitia in Gaul (now France), which took them farther eastward to the Alps. Imagine the five-year-old crossing the snowy mountains in his little Roman sandals, or maybe, if he was lucky, in a pair of *calagae* (the "little boots" that would one day give a still unborn emperor the nickname Caligula). Once across the Alps, it would have been southward to sunny Rome, a big, noisy city with chariots and carts and mules laden with gear, and as the boy set down his little *sacculum* to take it all in, he would have been far too young even to imagine the cruelties that lurked by firelight in that place.

Over the years, he received his education there in Rome, but as a young man, ill health drove him to Egypt, where his still devoted aunt resided with her husband, who was governor there. Modern researchers have identified Seneca's condition as either asthma, tuberculosis, or a mixture of the two. In a letter to a friend, he said that his condition was "well enough described as 'shortness of breath,'" explaining that like "a squall at sea" it never lasted much longer than an hour.[131] Still, when one is gasping for air with no medicine for relief, an hour can be a very long time.

Political Career

In AD 31, Seneca returned to Rome, entered politics, and began working his way up the ladder. Then suddenly in AD 38 he found himself out of favor with the emperor. Infamous for his injustices, Caligula ordered Seneca to be executed because, as Dio put it, "he pleaded a case well in the senate while the emperor was present."[132] A jealous fellow, was Caligula. Fortunately, his medical condition actually saved his life in this case because a woman was able to persuade Caligula that

Roman mosaic depicting a theatre mask

Seneca was in the advanced stages of tuberculosis and would die soon anyway. Fortunately, that turned out not to be true.

When Caligula was assassinated in AD 41, his uncle, Claudius, became the next emperor, and once again Seneca found himself out of favor. Accused of a love affair he probably did not have, Seneca was exiled to the island of Corsica for seven years, where he kept busy writing numerous works on philosophy and morality—and tragic plays. Fortunately, Agrippina, Claudius' wife, needed a reliable tutor for her twelve-year-old son Nero, so she prevailed upon Claudius to bring Seneca back to Rome. Nero, not yet the villain he was to become, must have taken a liking to his tutor because when he became the emperor of the Roman empire at age seventeen, he tapped Seneca to become one of his closest advisors. This was both the "good news" and the "bad news" for Seneca, because Agrippina (Rome's version of a "hover mother") was determined that her son listen to her, and not this stuffy philosopher. Nero resolved his problems with his mother by killing her, but Agrippina, as it turned out, was not easy to kill. It took shipwrecks, poison, and knives to do the poor woman in, but in the aftermath Nero felt he had to cover for his crime by accusing his mother of treason. That way, you see, she would have deserved what was coming to her. To this end, he called upon his word-weaver, Seneca, to ghost-write a letter explaining to the Senate why Agrippina's decease was so necessary to the health of the state. Only a fragment of this speech has survived to modern times, but Quintilian once included it in his rhetoric textbook as an example of excellence in sentence structure by means of doubling:

Salvum me esse adhuc nec credo nec gaudeo.

As yet I cannot believe or rejoice that I am safe. (Inst. Or. 8.5)

Writing Style

All of Seneca's tragedies were based on the Greek stories made so famous by Aristophanes, Sophocles, and Euripides, though he did add his distinctive touches to them. His style was very epigrammatic, that is, he had a knack for boiling down great truths into short, memorable lines. Look at these examples from *Hecuba:*

- Life bereft of honor is toil and trouble.

- I must do and dare, whether I win or lose.

- Numbers are a fearful thing and, joined to craft, a desperate foe.

- How can I escape reproach if I judge the "not guilty"?

Revenge Tragedies

Seneca is well known for his tragedies, especially *Medea, The Trojan Women,* and *Thyestes.* The specific genre perfected by Seneca is called today the *revenge tragedy*, a genre that later exercised great influence over Shakespeare and other English playwrights in the sixteenth and seventeenth centuries. The characteristics of a revenge tragedy are these:

1. A wrong has been committed against the hero—typically the murder of a family member or a friend.

2. A ghost appears and goads the hero into action.

3. Supernatural characters, such as gods, Furies, demons, and angels, have a role to play.

4. A prophecy or a curse may drive the action of the play.

5. There may be madness (or pretended madness).

6. Violent acts are part of the spectacle.

7. At the end of the play, the stage is strewn with bodies.

In a way, revenge is a sort of punishment, a subject that Seneca often wrote about in his essays; and, though he recognized the need for self-control in matters of punishment, he also recognized that rage sometimes prevented mere mortals from exercising it. "He who inflicts too great punishment comes very near to punishing unjustly,"[133] he wrote in *De Clementia* (On Mercy), and that point of view is often exhibited in his revenge plays as well.

The Christian Nexus

In the last years of the reign of Claudius, the Jews had been expelled from Rome, and we learn in the book of Acts that some of them, including the Roman Jewish Christians Priscilla and Aquila, made their way to the Greek city of Corinth. Interestingly, at about the same time he expelled the Jews, Claudius had sent Seneca's brother Gallio to be proconsul in Achaia, which meant that when the Jews in Corinth rose up against the teachings of Paul, Gallio was asked to hear their case. As Luke recorded in the book of Acts:

> But when Gallio was proconsul of Achaia, the Jews made a united attack on Paul and brought him before the tribunal, saying, "This man is persuading people to worship God contrary to the law." But when Paul was about to open his mouth, Gallio said to the Jews, "If it were a matter of wrongdoing or vicious crime, O Jews, I would have reason to accept your complaining. But since it is a matter of questions about words and names and your own law, see to it yourselves. I refuse to be a judge of these things. And he drove them from the tribunal. And they all seized Sosthenes, the ruler of the synagogue, and beat him in front of the tribunal. But Gallio paid no attention to any of this (18:12-17).

The apostle Paul is brought before Gallio, the brother of Seneca

Perhaps it would not be impossible to draw the conclusion from this narrative that Gallio heard the message of the Gospel at that time, right there in the tribunal. What he felt in his heart, we will never know, but since Seneca was in the heart of Rome at a time when the Christians were sharing the gospel with the Gentiles, one wonders if the two learned brothers ever discussed the ramifications of what they were hearing.

In the fourth century, some correspondence came to light which purported to be an exchange of letters between Seneca and Paul. That possibility has now been thoroughly debunked (the quality of the writing was too poor to be theirs, for one thing), yet it is still true that Seneca's writings do hauntingly echo the Christian worldview. That Seneca may well have heard the Christian narrative is certainly suggested in this passage from his essay *De Ira (On Anger)*:

> Behold the most glorious cities whose foundations can scarcely be traced — anger cast them down. Behold solitudes stretching lonely for many miles without a single dweller — anger laid them waste. Behold all the leaders who have been handed down to posterity as instances of an evil fate — anger stabbed this one in his bed, struck down this one amid the sanctities of the feast, tore this one to pieces in the very home of the law and in full view of the crowded forum, forced this one to have his blood spilled by the murderous act of his son, another to have his royal throat cut by the hand of a slave, *another to have his limbs stretched upon the cross* (emphasis added).[134]

Similarly, in his play *Hecuba,* Seneca penned this line for the Chorus: "From one man's folly came a universal curse, bringing death to the land of Simois, with trouble from an alien shore." This line is so close to that of Paul in his epistle to the Romans that one must wonder if Seneca had read it: "Therefore, just as sin came into the world through one man, and death through sin, and so death spread to all men because all sinned" (5:12). Paul's letter is believed to have been written to Gentile Christians in Rome between 55 and 57 AD, a time when Seneca is known to have been in Rome, tutoring Nero. Had someone shown it to him? Did he take it to heart?

Though not all agree, the manner of Seneca's death has led some to believe he was a believer at the end. Here's how it happened: In the year 65, an attempt was made on Nero's life. Nero, fixated on the idea that Seneca was a part of the conspiracy, ordered the philosopher to commit suicide. In his country house, with Roman guards looking on to ensure his compliance, Seneca proceeded to cut the veins in his legs, thinking he would bleed out. When that did not succeed, he took poison, and Tacitus tells the rest of the story:

> *Postremo stagnum calidae aquae introiit, respergens proximos servorum addita voce libare se liquorem illum Iovi liberatori. Exim balneo inlatus et vapore eius exanimatus.*

> At last he entered a pool of heated water, from which he sprinkled the nearest of his slaves, adding the exclamation, "I offer this liquid as a libation to Jupiter the Deliverer."[135]

He was then carried into a steaming bath, where he suffocated.

Centuries later, another poet, the Italian Boccaccio, concluded from this passage that Seneca was signaling a form of baptism in this manner of death. Boccaccio speculates:

> What is more, I am encouraged to hope for the best in regard to his salvation by one of the very last acts of his life. When he went to the bath, he said that he was offering the water he sprinkled to Jove Liberator. It strikes me that these words may be interpreted as follows. Despite having had that baptism of the faith that our theologians call 'flaminis,' Seneca, as far as we know, was not reborn according to the usual Christian custom of baptism through water and the Holy Spirit. We may say, then, that he sacrificed that water to Jove Liberator, *i.e.,* to Jesus Christ Who truly was the Liberator of humankind through His through his death and resurrection. (The fact that he uses the name Jove is of no consequence, for we earlier showed that name to be perfectly appropriate for God; in fact, it is appropriate for Him and for no other.) Therefore, we may interpret his act as bathing in that water and becoming a Christian, with the visual sacrament, just as he had already done mentally. Everyone may think whatever he likes on this subject.[136]

Confronted by the narrative of Christ, a theme which has appealed to dramatists down through the ages, the tragedian Seneca may have pondered its meaning. Seneca's tragic plays are often referred to as revenge tragedies, but in Christ's story, though there was injury, there was no revenge. "Father, forgive them," Jesus said. Was Boccaccio right? At the end, did Seneca find confirmation in the sacrifice of Christ for what he already had tried to say as a Stoic in his plays: that anger and unbridled revenge gain a person nothing?

One of the principles of Seneca's philosophy of Stocism [STŌ-ə-sĭ-zəm] was that the emotions needed to be controlled, yet he showed again and again in his plays how elusive self-control was, how anger led almost inevitably to madness and bloody revenge. Some have even wondered how a man with his particular views on ranging in the emotions could have written some of the things he did. Like Boccaccio, we can only hope that, by studying the Christian message, he found it a relief to find self-control to be a Fruit of the Spirit that was finally accessible to humankind through the sacrifice of Christ.

Plautus

The life of the dramatist Plautus (c. 254 BC- 184 BC) is in many ways like that of the American novelist Mark Twain (1835-1910).

- Both were born far from the centers of power (Twain in Missouri and Plautus in northeastern Italy).

- As young men, both worked in the practical, not the literary world (Twain as a riverboat pilot and Plautus as a stage carpenter).

**Titus Maccius Plautus
c. 254 BC – 184 BC**

- Both made business investments that did not pan out (Twain in a mechanical typesetter and Plautus in a nautical venture).

- Both used pseudonyms (Mark Twain being a pseudonym for Samuel Clemens and Plautus' name being a combination of characters' names, more of which later).

- Both lived during a time of war (Twain during the American Civil War and Plautus during the Second Punic War and the Macedonian Wars).

- Both were humorists (Twain evincing a wry humor and Plautus the broad laughter of situation comedy).

- Both wrote about the common people (Twain, the ordinary folk of the American South and Plautus, the stock characters of New Comedy).

- Both presented slaves in a positive light (Twain creating the character of the escaped slave Jim and Plautus, the bossy and shrewd Palaestrio).

- Both employed colloquial dialogue which is difficult to translate into other languages (Twain the regional dialect of his native Missouri and Plautus the slang-y style of Latin used by the common people).

- Both showed a bias against religion (Twain's "War Prayer" sharply criticizing Christians who favored military expansion and Plautus' mocking of the gods in a number of his plays).

- Both adapted their cultural heritage for audiences of their own place and time (Twain by using American values in *A Connecticut Yankee in King Arthur's Court* and *The Prince and the Pauper* and Plautus by Romanizing many of the Greek comedies of Menander).

- Both established themselves as giants in their literary tradition (Twain being called "the father of American literature" and Plautus, as the founder of the Roman dramatic tradition).

Plautus' Name

Plautus' full Latin name was Titus Maccius Plautus, but his *nomen* (Maccius) and his *cognomen* (Plautus) are thought to have been the equivalent of today's "stage names." The name Maccius, for example, was typically used for clowns in farces, and the name Plautus apparently meant "flat-footed." Whether the combination of these two words was a deliberate attempt by Plautus to poke fun at himself is anyone's guess.

No Politics?

A plebian himself, Plautus depicted the plebians as clever and easy to love. Since he was writing in the tradition of New Comedy, he wrote more about human situations than politics, which had been the focus of Old Comedy. The decision to take that direction may have been due, in part, to the fact that the Romans did not allow the same freedom of speech that the Greeks had enjoyed in the fifth century. In fact, at the time Plautus was just beginning to write, another playwright named Gnaeus Naevius was receiving punishment for sarcastic comments he had made about the ruling class in one of his plays. It would have been a cautionary piece of news to Plautus.

Still, scholar Andrew West believes that Plautus dipped his toes into the political waters in one of his plays, *Miles Glorious (The Braggart Soldier)*, which West believes contained a veiled reference to something going on in the Senate at the time.[137] Scipio Africanus, a general well loved by the people, was trying at the time to persuade the unwilling Senate to send a Roman army against Macedonia. The people were most definitely on his side, and a speech by Plautus' character Periplecomenus can be seen as the words of the plebian class to Scipio.

The plot runs thus: Periplecomenus, a young ambassador, is intent on separating his sweetheart from the clutches of his rival, who lives in an adjoining house. Unfortunately, he and the young lady are espied alone together in his home and must devise an explanation for their being together to protect the young lady from the villain's jealousy. The slave Palaestrio promises to solve the problem for his master, and Periplecomenus speeds the slave on with these encouraging words:

PERIPLECOMENUS
Don't you see that the enemy is upon you, and that siege is being laid to your back? Take counsel, then; obtain aid and assistance in this matter; the hastily, not the leisurely, is befitting here. Get the start of them in some way, and in some direction this moment lead around your troops. Close round the enemy in siege; prepare the convoy for our side. Cut off the enemy's provision, secure yourself a passage, by which supplies and provision may be enabled in safety to reach yourself and your forces. Look to this business; the emergency is sudden. Invent—contrive—this instant give us some clever plan; so that that which has been seen here within, may not have been seen; that which has been done, may not have been done. There, my man, you undertake a great enterprise; lofty the defenses which you erect. If you yourself alone but say you undertake this, I have a certainty that we are able to rout our foes.

PALAESTRIO
I do say so, and I do undertake it.

PERIPLECOMENUS
And I do pronounce that you shall obtain that which you desire.[138]

Was the sub-text here that the people wished to encouraged Scipio in his "siege" against the Senate and, eventually, in his siege against Macdeonia? West may be right that this speech was Plautus' indirect way of sneaking in some political commentary at a time when playwrights went about on thin ice.

Plautus' Influence

Throughout the Middle Ages, several Christian writers showed familiarity with Plautus' plays, among them Jerome, Augustine, and Bishop Sidonius Apollinaurus of Gaul. And, what is more, Plautus' staying power has been noted in England's Shakespeare, France's Molière, and America's Cole Porter. To be specific, Shakespeare's play *The Comedy of Errors* (c. 1585), which involved twins and mistaken identity, was an adaptation of Plautus' *Menaechimi*. And both Molière's *Amphitryon* (1668) and Porter's *Out of This World* (1950) were re-makes of Plautus' *Amphitruo*, which involved the antics of the god Jupiter.

Epitaph

Plautus' life came to a close at age 70 in 254 BC, and the epitaph he composed for himself was chiseled on his tomb:

Postquam est mortem aptus Plautus, Comoedia luget,
scaena est deserta, dein Risus, Ludus Iocusque
et Numeri innumeri simul omnes conlacrimarunt.

Since Plautus is dead, Comedy mourns,
Deserted is the stage; then Laughter, Jest and Wit,
And Melody's countless numbers all together wept.

EXERCISE 10.1: Analyzing a Character of Plautus

<u>Directions</u>: After reading the introduction to a monologue from *The Casket* by Plautus, read the monologue that follows. When finished, proceed to the questions, where you can analyze the character using the GOTE technique from Chapter 2.

Excerpt from *The Casket*
By Plautus

INTRODUCTION: *Halisca is a servant girl who has lost a box (a casket) which contained toys and trinkets found seventeen years previously with an infant girl who had been left for dead by an unmarried woman who could not take care of the baby. That girl, Silenum, is now seventeen, and her parents (now married) have learned that their daughter is still alive and are searching for her. The woman who raised Silenum is aware of the search and is willing to return the girl to her parents (perhaps for a reward).* *As the following scene opens, Halisca, who had been entrusted with the casket, realizes she has lost it and, along with it, the only means by which Silenum can be identified and reunited with her parents. Unbeknownst to Halisca, Silenum's birth mother, Phanostrata, and her slave Lampadio have not only found the casket Halisca dropped, but are following her in an effort to discover Silenum's whereabouts.*

HALISCA

If heaven doesn't rescue me, I'm dead and done for, with not a soul to look to for aid! Oh, how miserable my own heedlessness makes me! Oh! How I dread what will happen to my back, if my mistress finds out I've been so negligent! [*Thinking*] Surely I had that little casket in my hands and received it from her here in front of the house, and where it is now I don't know, unless I dropped it somewhere about here, as I suspect. [*To audience*] Dear gentlemen, dear spectators, do tell me if anyone of you saw him, the man who carried it off or who picked it up. Did he go [*Pointing*] this way, or that? [*Pauses, then indignantly*] I'm none the wiser for asking or pestering them—the creatures always enjoy seeing a woman in trouble! Now I'll [*Scans the ground*] examine the footprints here, in case I can find any. For if no one passed by after I went inside, the casket would be lying here. [*Looking about again, then hopelessly*] What am I to do? I'm done for, I fancy! It's all over, my day has come, unlucky, fated wretch that I am! Not a trace of it, and there won't be a trace left of me, either! It's lost, and so I'm lost, too! But I won't give up, though; I'll keep on looking. Oh, my heart's in a flutter and my back's in a fright—fear on both sides driving me frantic! What poor, poor things human beings are! Now he's happy, whoever he is, that has it—something that's no use to him and the death of me! But I'm delaying myself by not setting to work. To work, Halisca! Eyes on the ground, eyes down! Track it—sharp now—like an augur! [*Looks for footprints, her nose close to the ground*]

LAMPADIO

(*aside to Phanostrata*) Mistress!

PHANOSTRATA

Well? What is it?

LAMPADIO
She's the one!

PHANOSTRATA
What one?

LAMPADIO
That dropped the casket.

PHANOSTRATA
She certainly is. She's marking the place where she dropped it. It's plain enough.

HALISCA
But he went this way . . . Here's the mark of a shoe in the dust . . . I'll follow it up this way! Now here's where he stopped with someone else . . . Here's the scene of the fracas I saw a moment ago . . . No, he didn't go on this way . . . he stood here . . . from here he went over there . . . A consultation was held here . . . There are two people concerned, that's clear as day . . . Aha! Just one person's tracks! . . . He went this way, though . . . I'll investigate . . . From here he went over here . . . from here he went—[*after an energetic and futile search*] nowhere! [*With wry resignation*] It's no use. What's lost is lost—the casket and my cuticle together. I'm going back inside.[139]

GOTE

1. What is Halisca's goal?

2. What is the obstacle that prevents her from accomplishing her goal?

3. What tactics does she use to accomplish her goal?

4. What degree of expectation does she have that she will accomplish her goal?

Scrutinizing Roman Attitudes

Plautus' play *The Casket* concerns an aspect of Roman culture that deeply concerned the early Christians—infanticide. In the pagan culture of Greece and Rome, unwanted babies would typically be drowned or exposed in the wilderness to starve, become prey for wild animals, or perish from the extremes of temperature. Like Silenum in the play, most babies who were victims of such exposure were girls. The callous attitude of fathers toward their female children is shown in this line from a letter written from Roman Alexandria. The letter, which has been dated to June 17, 1 BC, was written by a man named Hilarion to his wife Alis, advising her that he would be staying on in Alexandria for a while. Then he casually adds: "If—good luck to you!—you bear offspring, if it is a male, let it live; if it is a female, expose it."[140] And the law did indeed give fathers the right to determine the fate of their children.

Plautus was writing about 200 years before the birth of Christ, but a comment by Seneca the Younger, who lived in the first century AD, shows the attitude the early Christians encountered: it was simply a way to rid the world of weaklings:

> We knock mad dogs on the head, we slaughter fierce and savage bulls, and we doom scabby sheep to the knife, lest they should infect our flocks: we destroy monstrous births, and we also drown our children if they are born weakly or unnaturally formed; to separate what is useless from what is sound is an act, not of anger, but of reason.[141]

Powerless and despised by the authorities, Christians were in no position to move the government to protect these children, but they did what they could in their own communities. For one thing, they provided Gentile converts to Christianity with a treatise, called the Didache, which imparted Christian ethics to new believers. The Didache clearly stated: "Thou shalt not procure abortion, nor commit infanticide."[142]

In addition, they often rescued exposed infants and raised them as their own. There was not much they could do in the way of the law until after Constantine became a Christian, but eventually they did triumph. The Justinian Code, for example, states: "Those who expose children, possibly hoping they would die, and those who use the potions of the abortionist are subject to the full penalty of the law — both civil and ecclesiastical — for murder. Should exposure occur, the finder of the child is to see to it that he is baptized and that he is treated with Christian care and compassion. They may be then adopted … even as we have been adopted into the Kingdom of grace."[143]

EXERCISE 10.2: Logic

<u>Directions</u>: Discuss these questions with your classmates.

1. Re-read the words of Seneca quoted from *Of Anger*. Discuss Seneca's idea in the light of the teaching found in Proverbs 14:12: "There is a way that seems right to a man, but its end is the way to death."

2. Construct a syllogism that underlies Seneca's comment. Discuss whether or not it is a sound argument.

   Major premise:_____

   Minor premise:_____

   Conclusion:_____

      Your observations: _____

3. Construct a syllogism that underlies the position of the Church. Discuss whether or not it is a sound argument.

   Major premise:_____

   Minor premise:_____

   Conclusion:_____

      Your observations: _____

Terence

"Homo sum, humani nil a me alienum puto."
"I am a man, I consider nothing that is human alien to me."
—Terence

So said Publius Terentius Afer (or Terence, as he is called in English) in the second century BC, and truly he was a man with insight into the human condition. Though he lived in pre-Christian times, his plays (all in the tradition of New Comedy) found a Christian audience in the medieval and Reformation eras.

Terence (d. 159 BC)

Who exactly was this man? To seek an answer, we can gather some clues from his name. Roman naming customs allowed three names for a male: the *praenomen* (Publius), the *nomen* (Terentius), and the *cognomen* (Afer). If Terence was a Roman himself, his family would have called him by his *praenomen*, Publius, while he was growing up. This was a typical name for a Roman boy. But his nomen and cognomen tell us other things about him. For one thing, Terence was a slave. His master was a Roman senator named Terentius Lucanus, who at some point recognized the lad's intelligence, saw to his education, and eventually set him free. Publius took his master's name, Terentius, as his nomen, perhaps in gratitude to a man who had treated him well. As for the cognomen, Afer, much ink has been spilled. Some believe this name suggests African origins, and, indeed Aelius Donatus, who wrote a commentary on Terence's plays in the fourth century, said that Terentius had an olive complexion, suggesting a north African origin such as Carthage or Libya. However, others point out that Afer was the name of a prominent plebian family in Rome, and since the cognomen was often used to refer to a particular branch of a large family, that party believes Terence was a Roman of the *gens* Domitia. How he came to be a slave is unknown, though if he were from north Africa, one can surmise that he or his ancestors were captured following a Roman military victory.

Terence was born sometime between 195 and 185 BC. His first comedy was performed in 170 BC, at which time he would have been fifteen years old if the later date of 185 BC is accurate. He did have a short life, dying at about age thirty-five while on a trip to Greece, but he still managed to write and present six plays during his short life. Terentius Lucanus may have introduced Terence to friends among the curule aediles, who were impressed enough to send him to the most famous playwright of the times, Caecilius Statius, for polishing. Before long, he went before some theatre judges, and we are told: "Unknown and meanly clad, Terence began to read from a low stool his opening scene, so often cited by Cicero as a model of narration. A few verses showed the elder poet that no ordinary writer was before him, and the young aspirant, then in his 27th year, was invited to share the couch and supper of his judge."[144]

Terence's rapid success earned him the envy of Luscius Lavinius, a mediocre poet who attacked Terence with charges of plagiarism and mishandling the plays of ancient Greece. Sometimes hoity-toity people have difficulty recognizing abilities in the less well-educated and, despite obvious proof of talent, will insist that such quality work could only have been done by their "betters." Terence, the former slave, was known to have had wealthy, educated friends who liked to meet and discuss intellectual matters, much in the way that C. S. Lewis and the Inklings did in twentieth-century London. Luscius spread rumors that it was these elites who had really written Terence's plays. Most have considered Luscius' charges to be false, but Terence never directly denied the charge. However, if Terence were indeed from north Africa, Latin would not have been his native tongue. His excellent command of Latin has long been acclaimed, but if it were his second language, it is possible that he asked for advice from native speakers from time to time. This would be classified as editing, not plagiarism.

Proof of Terence's mastery of Latin lies in the fact that throughout the Middle Ages, the plays of Terence were used in European monasteries and convents for the teaching of Latin. This means that one of the most eloquent Fathers of the Christian Church, Jerome (AD 347-420), whose native tongue was the Illyrian dialect of Slovenia, had cut his teeth on Terence's Latin at the age of twelve when he was sent to Rome for an education. In fact, Jerome's tutor in Rome was Aelius Donatus, who was writing about the works of Terence at the time, so it is reasonable to conclude that Donatus used Terence's Latin plays to instruct young Jerome. In later years, Jerome commented on Terence's translation skills,

praising him for "preserving the beauty and charm" of the original Greek plays he translated.

The Reformation figure, Martin Luther, whose native tongue was German, was also quite familiar with the works of Terence and once used Terence's character Gnatho to make a point, calling him "an ear-scratcher, a dissembler, a trencher-licker, one that talketh for his belly's sake, and is altogether a man-pleaser," adding, "This is a sin of mankind, whose intent is to get all they can though others are hurt thereby."[145]

To clarify, Gnatho is a good example of the stock character called a "parasite," a person who mooches off of others. For a peek into Gnatho's thinking, look at the lines that Terence wrote for him to say about the "art" of mooching:

GNATHO
As I was, coming along to-day, I met a certain person of this place, of my own rank and station, no mean fellow, one who, like myself, had guttled away his paternal estate; I saw him, shabby, dirty, sickly, beset with rags and years. "What's the meaning of this garb?" said I; he answered, "Because, wretch that I am, I've lost what I possessed: see to what I am reduced—all my acquaintances and friends forsake me." On this I felt contempt for him in comparison with myself. "What!" said I, "You pitiful sluggard. Have you so managed matters as to have no hope left? Have you lost your wits together with your estate? Don't you see me, who have risen from the same condition? What a complexion I have, how spruce and well dressed, what portliness of person? I have everything, yet have nothing; and although I possess nothing, still, of nothing am I in want." "But I," said he, "unhappily, can neither be a butt nor submit to blows." "What!" said I, "Do you suppose it is managed by those means? You are quite mistaken. Once upon a time, in the early ages, there was a calling for that class; this is a new mode of coney-catching [scamming].[6] I, in fact, have been the first to strike into this path. There is a class of men who strive to be the first in everything, but are not; to these I make my court; I do not present

___
[6] Scamming, being a con artist

192

myself to them to be laughed at; but I am the first to laugh with them, and at the same time to admire their parts: whatever they say, I commend; if they contradict that self-same thing, I commend again. Does anyone deny? I deny: does he affirm? I affirm: in fine, I have so trained myself as to humor them in everything. This calling is now by far the most productive. . . . While we were thus talking, in the meantime we arrived at the market-place. Overjoyed, all the confectioners ran at once to meet me; fishmongers, butchers, cooks, sausage-makers, and fishermen, whom, both when my fortunes were flourishing and when they were ruined, I had served, and often serve still. They complimented me, asked me to dinner, and gave me a hearty welcome. When this poor hungry wretch saw that I was in such great esteem, and that I obtained a living so easily, then the fellow began to entreat me that I would allow him to learn this method of me; I bade him become my follower if he could; as the disciples of the Philosophers take their names from the Philosophers themselves, so too, the Parasite ought to be called Gnathonics.

PARMENO
(Apart to the audience.) Do you see the effects of ease and feeding at another's cost?[146]

Certainly Martin Luther recognized Gnatho as the kind of person Paul had counseled the Corinthians about when he had written, "If anyone is not willing to work, let him not eat" (2 Thess. 3:10a). Thus, we may conclude that Terence was right when he said that nothing in human experience was alien to him. Though he died 200 years before the birth of Christ, he knew of the sin nature; he just did not know of the Savior.

THE RHETORIC OF ROMAN PLAYS

Chapter 11

Introduction

As in Greece, lessons in rhetoric in ancient Rome began with instruction in the progymnasmata before moving on into advanced oratory. Therefore, once again, we can expect to find evidence of the progymnasmata in the works of Roman authors. In addition to guidance in argumentation, classical students learned how to enrich their diction with figures of speech (tropes), syntax (sentence structure), and word choice. The purpose of this chapter is to explore these elements in Roman plays.

Progymnasmata: Comparison (*Synkrisis*)

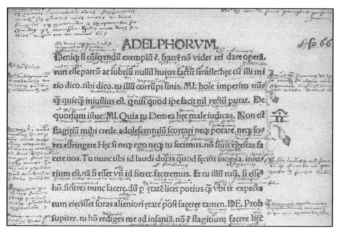

Annotated page of Terence's *Adelphoe* (act one, scene two) in Latin

In *Adelphoe (The Brothers)* by the Roman playwright Terence, we see the progymnasmata element of Comparison as the first speech after the prologue, when one Micio comes onstage and speaks to his slave, Storax. In this monologue, the audience (along with Storax) is given a comparison between Micio and his brother Demea. Before examining the speech itself, let us begin with a review of the two patterns of a standard comparison. (Note: The terms *comparison* and *contrast* are used interchangeably in discussions of this progymnasmata element.)

The first option for presenting a comparison is a point-by-point fashion. For an example, let's return to Greek literature and draw a comparison between the comedies of Aristophanes and Menander. We could isolate three features—say, characters, subject matter, and tone—and address them one by one (or point by point, if you will). The contrasts will be nailed down by using either a coordinating conjunction such as *but, however,* or *on the other hand* or a subordinating conjunction such as *while* or *whereas.* The finished product would look like this:

> The comedies of Aristophanes are different from those of Menander in several ways. With regard to characters, those of Aristophanes were normally gods and heroes, *but* those of Menander were ordinary people. With regard to subject matter, Aristophanes wrote about politics and great events; Menander, *on the other hand,* wrote about everyday life. With regard to tone, Aristophanes' characters frequently employed sarcasm *while* Menander's characters spoke in a more light-hearted way.

The other way to present a comparison is to use a block pattern. That is to say, when comparing Aristophanes and Menander, one complete paragraph can be given over to Aristophanes and then another paragraph to Menander. The opening sentence would express the topic, and the second paragraph would begin with a transition such as *on the other hand* or *in contrast* to move the reader (or listener) into the second block. The pattern would look like this:

> The comedies of Aristophanes are different from those of Menander. Aristophanes wrote about gods and heroes, focusing on cosmic issues such as a descent into Hades, or political matters, such as the behavior of the reigning tyrant. Because Aristophanes was poking fun at these normally dignified characters, he employed sarcasm to throw his punches.

> *In contrast,* Menander wrote about everyday people in everyday situations. His characters might be soldiers, maidens, or slaves. Instead of having a political agenda, as Aristophanes did, Menander simply hoped to entertain. Therefore, the tone of his plays is more light-hearted.

Notice in this example that, except for the topic sentence, information about Menander does not appear in the first block, which is about Aristophanes. However, in the second block, which belongs to Menander, some specific contrasts with Aristophanes are highlighted.

Now, the rhetoric teachers of antiquity advised that when making a comparison for the purpose of persuasion, the writer (or speaker) should make clear which of the two subjects in the comparison is better. In other words, instead of being a simple listing of differences, as in the examples above, a comparison should put one of the subjects in a positive light and one in a more negative light. Therefore, if one preferred the plays of Menander, the passage would look more like this:

> For a student performance, the comic plays of Menander are *preferable to* those of Aristophanes. For one thing, the characters of Menander are more like those that students encounter in everyday life—their parents, siblings, teachers, and friends, while those of Aristophanes often have superhuman supernatural qualities. It is harder for an audience to identify with those. Furthermore, the tone of Menander's plays is more light-hearted, evoking chuckles and gentle laughter, while the tone of Aristophanes' plays is sarcastic and mean-spirited. The laughter of the audience at a play by Aristophanes is more derisive and jeering, and does not elevate the spirit. Therefore, it *would be better* for students to perform a comedy by Menander than by Aristophanes.

The examples above are all in expository style like that used in textbooks, but in a dramatic style, the actor will be working with the more fluid, colloquial style of conversation. The inflection of the voice will depend on the circumstances—the relationship between the two characters, the character's individual persona, the subject matter at hand, and the setting, for example. The actor and director will work together so that the comparison lies less in structure words like *however* and *whereas* than in voice inflection on, say, the names of the characters or the pronouns that refer to them. For example, the voice would "jump up" on the bold-faced pronouns in a line such as, "**You**, my friend, always look at the dark cloud. You should try being more like **me** for a change. **I** always look for the silver lining."

The purpose of the exercise which follows is to provide the opportunity for you to examine this type of comparison, as it was handled in a play by Terence. As you read, please keep in mind that the writer composed this piece as an adult who had moved beyond the simple progymnasmata exercise that he had begun with as a child. Therefore, one finds more complexity with multiple comparisons going on in the same passage. It is an excellent example of where the early exercises can lead a talented student.

EXERCISE 11.1: Comparison in *The Brothers*

<u>Directions:</u> Please begin by reading a monologue from *The Brothers* by Terence, which presents a contrast between Micio and his brother Demea. It has been divided into numbered segments in order to facilitate analysis. After reading the excerpt, please answer the questions which follow.

The Brothers (Act 1, Scene 1)
By Terence

Enter MICIO, calling to a servant within.

MICIO
[1] Storax! Aeschinus has not returned home from the entertainment last night, nor any of the servants who went to fetch him.

[2] (*To himself*) Really, they say it with reason, if you are absent anywhere, or if you stay abroad at any time, 'twere better for that to happen which your wife says against you, and which in her passion she imagines in her mind, than the things which fond parents fancy. A wife, if you stay long abroad, either imagines that you are in love or are beloved, or that you are drinking and indulging your inclination, and that you only are taking your pleasure, while she herself is miserable. As for myself, in consequence of my son not having returned home, what do I imagine? In what ways am I not disturbed? For fear lest he may either have taken cold, or have fallen down somewhere, or have broken some limb.

[3] Oh dear! that any man should take it into his head, or find out what is dearer to him than he is to himself! And yet he is not my son, but my brother's. He is quite different in disposition. I, from my very youth upward, have lived a comfortable town life, and taken my ease; and, what they esteem a piece of luck, I have never had a wife. He, on the contrary to all this, has spent his life in the country, and has always lived laboriously and penuriously. He married a wife, and has two sons. This one, the elder of them, I have adopted. I have brought him up from an infant, and considered and loved him as my own.

[4] In him I centre my delight; this object alone is dear to me. On the other hand, I take all due care that he may hold me equally dear.

[5] I give—I overlook; I do not judge it necessary to exert my authority in everything; in fine, the things that youth prompts to, and that others do unknown to their fathers, I have used [accustomed] my son not to conceal from me. For he, who, as the practice is, will dare to tell a lie to or to deceive his father, will still more dare to do so to others. I think it better to restrain children through a sense of shame and liberal treatment, than through fear.

 [6] On these points my brother does not agree with me, nor do they please him. He often comes to me exclaiming, "What are you about, Micio? Why do you ruin for us this youth? Why does he intrigue? Why does he drink? Why do you supply him with the means for these goings on? You indulge him with too much dress; you are very inconsiderate." He himself is too strict, beyond what is just and reasonable; and he is very much mistaken, in my opinion, at all events, who thinks that an authority is more firm or more lasting which is established by force, than that which is founded on affection.

[7] Such is my mode of reasoning; and thus do I persuade myself. He, who, compelled by harsh treatment, does his duty, so long as he thinks it will be known, is on his guard: if he hopes that it will be concealed, he again returns to his natural bent. He whom you have secured by kindness, acts from inclination; he is anxious to return like for like; present and absent, he will be the same.

[8] This is the duty of a parent, to accustom a son to do what is right rather of his own choice, than through fear of another. In this the father differs from the master: He who cannot do this, let him confess that he does not know how to govern children.

[9] But is not this the very man of whom I was speaking? Surely it is he. I don't know why it is I see him out of spirits; I suppose he'll now be scolding as usual. Demea, I am glad to see you well.[147]

Questions:

1. Moving between Segments 1 and 2, what difference in voice modulation (loudness) might be required. Base your answer on the stage directions.

2. In Segment 2:

    a. Though Micio uses himself as an example, what two types of people is he comparing?

    b. What does he say is the difference between these two types of people when their loved one does not come home on time?

    c. What words would require voice inflection (for emphasis) to help convey the comparison and the varying underlying emotions of the two types?

    d. What gestures might help with the characterization and point Micio is making?

3. In Segment 3:

    a. What two pronouns carry the comparison along?

    b. What inflections might be necessary to convey the idea that Micio thinks his own life is better?

4. In Segment 4, Micio's lines include the transition *on the other hand*. This transition seems to imply a comparison, but a comparison is not readily apparent. Why do you think the lines employ such a structure? What might be going on in Micio's mind?

5. Segments 5 and 6 serve as a block comparison.

   a. Which of the brothers is described in Segment 5? in Segment 6?

   b. As in other places in the monologue, Terence layers comparisons here. Though the two paragraphs are a block comparison of the brothers, there is another comparison mentioned in Segment 5. What two types of people are compared there? Explain the difference between them.

   c. What blocking might be appropriate as Micio moves from Segment 5 to Segment 6?

6. In your own words, summarize the comparison made in Segment 7.

7. In Segment 8, Terence added yet another comparison.

   a. To whom does Micio compare the strict parent and the gentler parent?

b. The rhetoric teachers advised students not just to describe the two subjects, but to evaluate them. Has Terence accomplished that goal in this passage? Explain your answer.

8. In Segment 9, the actor would need to change the tone and pitch of his voice as Demea makes his entrance. What suggestions would you make to the actor playing this part?

Diction

Diction can be defined as the artistic use of language. In this section, three particular aspects of diction will be examined—tropes (figures of speech), syntax (sentence structure), and word choice.

Tropes

Tropes are figures of speech which writers can use to enrich the diction of their works. Most of them have Greek or Latin names because they were invented by the classical authors. Below are some of the tropes which Seneca the Younger used, along with examples from his play *Thyestes*.

1. **Anastrophe** (inverted word order)

    "O'er all his body a fleece of spun gold hangs."

    [Normal order: A fleece of spun gold hangs o'er all his body."]

2. **Anaphora** (repetition of the front part of a sentence for artistic effect)

    "*I long to* utter ill-omened lamentation, *I long to* rend these garments, rich dyed with Tyrian purple, *I long to* shriek aloud."[148]

3. **Epigram** (concise, insightful saying; adage)

   "Honour, virtue, faith are the goods of common men; let kings go where they please."

4. **Prosopopoeia** (personification)

   "*Night*, heavy with black, Tartarean fogs, *give ear unto my cries.*"

5. **Simile** (comparison using *like, as, more than*, or *less than*)

   "The slippery Serpent which, gliding *like a river*, separates the Bears, shall fall."

Syntax

In addition to the use of specific tropes, talented writers, such as Seneca, have such a good command of their language that they can manipulate the syntax (structure) of a sentence for artistic effect. The translator, of course, has the job of not only conveying the meaning of the lines, but also maintaining the author's distinct artistic style. Some examples from Seneca's *Thyestes* are these:

6. **Elliptical construction by gapping** (omitting words to avoid needless repetition)

   "Now enough time has been given to tables, *enough to wine.*"

7. **Parallelism** (repetition of a sentence pattern for artistic effect)

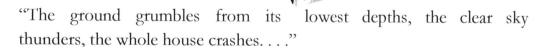

   "The ground grumbles from its lowest depths, the clear sky thunders, the whole house crashes. . . ."

8. **Participial adjectives** (*-ing, -ed*) in attributive position (in front of the noun)

   "new-crowned kings"

   "my tattling tongue"

9. **Participial phrases** (*-ing, -ed*) as adjectives immediately following the noun

"sceptres *wreathed with gold*"

"with hair *dripping with liquid nard*"

Word Choice

Mark Twain once said, "The difference between the right word and the almost right word is the difference between the lightning and the lightning bug." This adage expresses the idea that the best writers will also be talented with respect to word choice.

10. **Precise adjectives**

"It urges on my *sluggish* hands." [Better than *slow*]

". . . brandishing her torches *twain*." [Better than *two*]

11. **Verbs which express motion**

"Let him *spew forth* his hateful soul."

"Thou *shrinkest back*, my soul."

"With drawn sword, *rush* upon me."

"First *throw* thy house into confusion dire."

"A frantic tumult *shakes* and *heaves* deep my heart."

EXERCISE 11.2: Diction in *Thyestes*

<u>Directions</u>: Below is an excerpt from a tragedy entitled *Thyestes*, written by Seneca and translated into English by Frank Justus Miller. The play is a revenge tragedy about a man who takes vengeance by killing his rival's sons and serving them up as a cannibalistic meal. It has been divided into segments in order to isolate certain

features of diction.   As you read, keep in mind the accomplishment not only of Seneca, but also the translator, Miller, whose job was to render beautiful Greek into beautiful English. After reading the excerpt, complete the questions that follow by examining tropes, stylistic syntax, and word choice.

Thyestes (Act 3)
By Seneca the Younger
Translated by Frank Justus Miller

CHORUS:

[1] This sudden lull out of so great uproar what god has wrought?

[2] But now throughout Mycenae the arms of civil strife resounded; pale mother held fast their sons, the wife feared for her lord full armed, when to his hand came the reluctant sword, foul with the rust of peace.

[3] One strove to repair tottering walls, one to strengthen towers, crumbling with long neglect; another strove to shut gates tight with iron bars, while on the battlements the trembling guard kept watch o'er the troubled night—

[4] for worse than war is the very fear of war.

[5] Now the sword's dire threats have fallen; now still is the deep trumpet-blare; now silent the shrill clarion's blast; deep peace to a glad city is restored.

Theatre mask as part of theatre decoration at Ostia Antica, Rome, Italy

[6] So when the floods heave up from the ocean's depths and Corus lashes the Bruttian waters; when Scylla roars in her disturbed cavern, and mariners in harbour tremble at the sea which greedy Charybdis drains and vomits forth again; when the wild Cyclops, sitting on burning Aetna's crag, dreads his sire's rage, lest the o'erweening waves put out the fires that roar in immemorial furnaces; and when beggared Laërtes thinks, while Ithaca reels beneath the shock, that his kingdom may be submerged—then, if their strength has failed the winds,

[7] the sea sinks back more peaceful than a pool; and the deep waters which the ship feared to cleave, now far and wide studded with bellying sails, a beauteous sight, to pleasure-boats spread out their waves; and you may now count the fish swimming far below, where but lately beneath the mighty hurricane the tossed Cyclads trembled at the sea.

Questions:

NOTE: In the space provided, provide the sentence number where the trope is found and a few key words to identify it. The first one serves as an example.

I. Tropes

1. **Anastrophe** (inverted word order)

   1 - This sudden lull . . . wrought?

2. **Anaphora** (repetition of the front part of a sentence for artistic effect)

   a. Adverbial clauses

   b. Adverbs of time

3. **Epigram** (wise saying, adage)

4. **Prosopopoeia** (personification)

5. **Simile** (comparison *using like, as, more than*, or *less than*)

II. Syntax

6. **Elliptical construction by gapping** (omitting a verb to avoid needless repetition)

7. **Parallelism** (repetition of a sentence pattern for artistic effect)

8. **Participial adjectives** (*-ing, -ed*) in attributive position (in front of the noun)

9. **Participial phrases** (*-ing, -ed*) as adjectives (immediately following the noun)

III. Word Choice

10. **Colorful verbs which express motion**

    a. Segment 6 (five examples)

    b. Segment 7 (five examples)

11. **Precise adjectives**

12. ASSESSMENT: Having examined this passage for figures of speech, stylistic techniques, and word choice, how would you describe Seneca's writing style?

ACTIVITY: Vacation Simile Game

<u>Directions</u>: Choose four students for each round. One is the storyteller, who is presenting a slideshow to the audience with pictures of his or her recent vacation. The other three are the "pictures" in the slideshow. The game proceeds in this manner:

- The storyteller stands downstage right while the other three students stand upstage center

- The storyteller takes about 15 seconds to begin telling about where he or she went on vacation. Meanwhile, the other three students are adopting poses, frozen in position, representing something or someone in the storyteller's slides. The grander the pose, the better.

- The storyteller then turns around to look at the "picture" and, in an impromptu manner, uses similes to describe the "slides": "She was as snooty as a princess." "He had a smile like Count Dracula's."

- This repeats three more times until the storyteller ends the story about his or her "vacation."

ROMAN THEATRE TIDBITS FROM PRIMARY SOURCES

Chapter 12

The Theatre at Jerusalem

Coin from the time of Herod the Great, Greek letter Chi visible

In 27 BC, King Herod allowed the building of a theatre and an amphitheatre in Jerusalem and decorated it with the trophies of war the Romans had taken in their conquests—"all made of the purest gold and silver." This, together with the slaughter of men by lions and other beasts in the amphitheatre outraged the Jews. In their opinion, Herod had "revolted from the laws of his country, and corrupted their ancient constitution, by the introduction of foreign practices."[149] In what has come to be called the "trophies incident," they demanded that Herod take down the trophies, which they deemed to be false idols. Herod took some of the Jewish leaders with him to the theatre, had the trophies removed from the posts that supported them, and showed them that they were not statues (or idols), just shields and other spoils of war. This satisfied some of the crowd, but not all, and soon an assassination plot was afoot. Josephus, a Romanized Jewish historian, left an account of what happened and made clear that the assassination unfolded at the theatre:

Flavius Josephus (AD 37 – c. AD 100) author of *Antiquities of the Jews*

When they had taken this resolution [to assassinate Herod], and that by common consent, they went into the theatre, hoping that, in the first place, Herod himself could not escape them, as they should fall upon him so unexpectedly; and supposing, however, that if they missed him, they should kill a great many of those that were about him; and this resolution they took, though they should die for it, in order to suggest to the king what injuries he had done to the multitude. These conspirators, therefore, standing thus prepared beforehand, went about their design with great alacrity; but there was one of those spies of Herod, that were appointed for such purposes, to fish out and inform him of any conspiracies that should be made against him, who found out the whole affair, and told the king of it, as he was about to go into the theatre. So when he reflected on the hatred which he knew the greatest part of the people bore him, and on the disturbances that arose upon every occasion, he thought this plot against him not to be improbable. Accordingly,

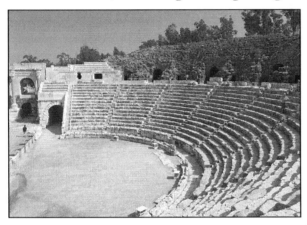

The Roman theatre at Jerusalem no longer exists, but this theatre at Beit Shean (23 miles southeast of Nazareth) may represent the architectural type in the region.

he retired into his palace and called those that were accused of this conspiracy before him by their several names; and as, upon the guards falling upon them, they were caught in the very fact, and knew they could not escape, they prepared themselves for their ends with all the decency they could, and so as not at all to recede from their resolute behavior, for they showed no shame for what they were about, nor denied it; but when they were seized, they showed their daggers, and professed that the conspiracy they had sworn to was a holy and pious action; that what they intended to do was not for gain, or out of any indulgence to their passions, but principally for those common customs of their country, which all the Jews were obliged to observe, or to die for them. This was what these men said, out of their undaunted courage in this conspiracy. So they were led away to execution by the king's guards that stood about them, and patiently underwent all the torments inflicted on them till they died. Nor was it long before that spy who had discovered them was seized on by some of the people, out of the hatred they bore to him; and was not only slain by them, but pulled to pieces, limb from limb, and given to the dogs. This execution was seen by many of the citizens, yet would not one of them discover the doers of it, till upon Herod's making a strict scrutiny after them, by bitter and severe tortures, certain women that were tortured confessed what they had seen done; the authors of which fact were so terribly punished by the king, that their entire families were destroyed for this their rash attempt; yet did not the obstinacy of the people, and that undaunted constancy they showed in the defense of their laws, make Herod any easier to them, but he still strengthened himself after a more secure manner, and resolved to encompass the multitude every way, lest such innovations should end in an open rebellion.[150]

The Theatre at Ephesus

The theatre at Ephesus in modern Turkey
Courtesy of Thomas Brosnahan, Turkey Travel Planner

About thirty years after the commotion in Jerusalem, another provocation led to a tumultuous episode at the theatre of Ephesus, preserved in the historical record by the apostle Luke in the nineteenth chapter of Acts.

The image of the theatre provides an idea of what seafarers would first have seen of Ephesus upon leaving the Aegean harbor and walking toward the city. Even in the picture, it exudes a palpable sense of death, a reminder that in Roman times, the theatres were given over largely to the carnage of the *bestiarii* and the gladiator games.

Indeed, in 2007, a gladiator graveyard was discovered nearby, containing the skeletons of about sixty-seven men, ranging in age from about twenty to thirty.[151]

The theatre at Ephesus was already about 340 years old when the events described in Acts 19 took place. The *basileus* (or king) Lysimachus, who died in 281 BC, is generally credited with calling for the construction of a Greek theatre after Alexander the Great had brought Hellenistic culture into Asia Minor. However, since no artifacts dated earlier than 100 BC have been discovered there, it probably was not finished until the passage of sixty years spent digging out a *cavea* in the slope of Mount Pion (now Panayir dagi).[152] It rose to a height of 100 feet and was paved with marble, as was the road that led to it from the agora. Once Roman concrete came into use, a third tier was added that did not require support from the mountain.

It would have been a familiar sight to Paul, who had spent three years in Ephesus, conversing first with the Jews in the synagogue and then with the Gentiles in the lecture hall of Tyrannus, who may have been a schoolmaster.[153] Luke did not record that Paul ever preached in the theatre, but Paul may well have steered clear of it since, in Greco-Roman fashion, it was devoted to a pagan deity and supported by the treasury of the temple.

The deity in this case was Artemis (Diana), and Ephesus had not only a sizable temple devoted to her, but a number of silversmiths busy churning out shrines and statuettes for what we might call today the "tourist trade." The festival of Artemis, held in the spring of the year, attracted thousands who wished to participate in the games and attend performances at the theatre and who, no doubt, purchased the silver works to take home with them.

In 57 AD, however, business was down, and anxiety had set in amongst the silversmiths whose livelihood—and religion—were at risk. One silversmith by the name of Demetrius was so upset that he called together a meeting of his fellow metal workers and presented them with this argument:

> Men, you know that from this business we have our wealth. And you see and hear that not only in Ephesus but in almost all of Asia this Paul has persuaded and turned away a great many people, saying that gods made with hands are not gods. And there is danger not only that this trade of ours may come into disrepute but also that the temple of the great goddess Artemis may be counted

as nothing, and that she may even be deposed from her magnificence, she whom all Asia and the world worship. When they heard this they were enraged and were crying out, "Great is Artemis of the Ephesians!" So the city was filled with the confusion, and they rushed together into the theater, dragging with them Gaius and Aristarchus, Macedonians who were Paul's companions in travel (Acts 19:25-27).

Assuming the gathering of the *argentarii* was in the commercial agora where they would normally have carried on their trade, one can see from the map below that it was not a long walk to the theatre, and the crowd grew bigger as it went along.

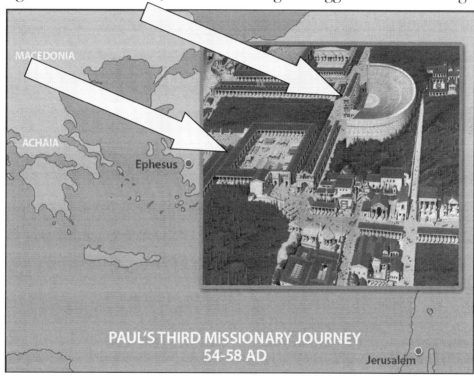

Top arrow points to the theatre; bottom arrow, to the agora, where the silversmiths, as well as the tentmakers Priscilla, Aquila, and Paul, conducted their trade.

"Now some cried out one thing, some another, for the assembly was in confusion, and most of them did not know why they had come together," said Luke (19:32).

Paul was not amongst the throng, as officials friendly to him had warned him "not to venture into the theatre," but two of his companions were dragged there, Gaius and Aristarchus, who were Macedonians. In addition, there were some Ephesian Jews in the crowd, and they nudged one of their fellows, Alexander, to go forward, perhaps to the stage, and address the crowd; and Alexander, Luke says, motioned with his hand and "wanted to make a defense to the crowd." However, "when they recognized that he was a Jew, for about two hours they all cried out with one voice, 'Great is Artemis of the Ephesians!'" (34).

Two hours! That is probably a longer time than they ever sat in the theatre for a play.

Finally, a town clerk was able to calm the mob, assured them that Paul and his companions were "neither sacrilegious nor blasphemers of our goddess," and suggested they take their legal complaint, if they had one, to the courts or the regular assembly. The crowd drifted away. And as Stephen Vincent Benét said about the taking of old John Brown, perhaps was heard "that huge sigh of a crowd turning back into men."[154]

 "After the uproar ceased, Paul sent for the disciples, and after encouraging them, he said farewell and departed for Macedonia" (20:1).

One final thought remains: Demetrius' apparent comfort with the theatre, where he directed the ranting crowd, combined with his obvious powers of rhetoric makes one wonder if the silversmith himself was an amateur actor, perhaps one of the locals who performed in the Roman Empire's version of "community theatre." But whether or not that is so, the theatre at Ephesus certainly played its own role in history in 57 AD when the past collided with the future within its precincts.

The Emperor Nero's Obsession

The Emperor Nero (37 AD-68 AD), infamous as the persecutor of Christians in the Colosseum at Rome, tried to make himself the darling of the theatrical communities in the Empire. In the next generation, the historian Suetonius wrote an account of Nero's obsession with the theatre in his "Life of Nero." Suetonius explained how Nero took lessons from the the master lyre-player and music tutor Terpnus but would not undergo the rigorous training that was necessary to create a strong voice. Suetonius describes his first performances this way:

> Finally encouraged by his progress, although his voice was weak and husky, he began to long to appear on the stage, and every now and then in the presence of his intimate friends he would quote a Greek proverb meaning "Hidden

music counts for nothing." And he made his début at Naples, where he did not cease singing until he had finished the number which he had begun, even though the theatre was shaken by a sudden earthquake shock. In the same city

Remains of the Roman theatre at Naples, site of a performance by Nero.

he sang frequently and for several days . . . . He was greatly taken too with the rhythmic applause of some Alexandrians, who had flocked to Naples from a fleet that had lately arrived, and summoned more men from Alexandria. Not content with that, he selected some young men of the order of knights and more than five thousand sturdy young commoners, to be divided into groups and learn the Alexandrian styles of applause (they called them "the bees," "the roof-tiles," and "the bricks"), and to ply them vigorously whenever he sang. These men were noticeable for their thick hair and fine apparel; their left hands were bare and without rings, and the leaders were paid four hundred thousand sesterces each."[155]

Suetonius also revealed how Nero's audience was not nearly as impressed with his talent he was:

> While he was singing no one was allowed to leave the theatre even for the most urgent reasons. And so it is said that some women gave birth to children there, while many who were worn out with listening and applauding, secretly leaped from the wall, since the gates at the entrance were closed, or feigned death and were carried out as if for burial.[156]

Suetonius also gives us a glimpse into Nero's manipulation of the judges and other performers:

> The trepidation and anxiety with which he took part in the contests, his keen rivalry of his opponents and his awe of the judges, can hardly be credited. As if his rivals were of quite the same station as himself, he used to show respect to them and try to gain their favour, while he slandered them behind their backs, sometimes assailed them with abuse when he met them, and even bribed those who were especially proficient.

Before beginning, he would address the judges in the most deferential terms, saying that he had done all that could be done, but the issue was in the hands of Fortune; they however, being men of wisdom and experience, ought to exclude what was fortuitous. When they bade him take heart, he withdrew with greater confidence, but not even then without anxiety, interpreting the silence and modesty of some as sullenness and ill-nature, and declaring that he had his suspicions of them. . . .

In competition he observed the rules most scrupulously, never daring to clear his throat and even wiping the sweat from his brow with his arm. Once indeed, during the performance

NERO, AND THE BURNING OF ROME.

Depiction of Nero singing and playing the lyre while Rome burns, by M. de Lipman.

of a tragedy, when he had dropped his sceptre but quickly recovered it, he was terribly afraid that he might be excluded from the competition because of his slip, and his confidence was restored only when his accompanist swore that it had passed unnoticed amid the delight and applause of the people. When the victory [of Nero] was won, he made the announcement himself; and for that reason he always took part in the contests of the heralds.[157]

But Nero, though he loved to take the prize himself, did not actually honor true talent, as Suetonius explains:

To obliterate the memory of all other victors in games and leave no trace of them, their statues and busts were all thrown down by his order, dragged off with hooks, and cast into privies.[158]

Charles Dickens at the Colosseum

The Roman Empire mutilated the theatre. They inherited from the Greeks a grand tradition—theatres that were architectural wonders, dramas so insightful of the human condition that they have lasted 2,500 years and been translated into virtually every tongue. But Rome took this and turned it over to stage executions, alligators and gladiators, and hungry people who could forget their hunger for an hour if only they could watch a brave man die and see his blood spill out into the sand. The stage performances were so degraded the pagan emperor himself had to run the actors out of town, and the mime plays were only redeemed by the true salvation discovered in the false baptisms on the stage, though followed as they were by torture and execution. It is no wonder that the theatre died for several hundred years to be revived ultimately by the Christian church, who cleansed it and made it an instrument of the Great Commission.

In 1749, Pope Benedict XIV pronounced the Colosseum a sacred site and installed stations of the cross around the arena, with a new cross in its center. But its old pagan power does not want to let go and can still oppress the hearts of those who wander there. Edgar Allan Poe in his play *Politan: A Tragedy,* written in 1833, expressed it well: "I feel ye now—I feel ye in your strength!" And Poe was not alone. In the eighteenth and nineteenth centuries, once history had reached a place where wealth and leisure permitted it, Europeans and Americans took to traveling to see the ancient places they had read of in their schoolbooks, and the Colosseum became the great attraction of those who wended their way to Rome.

Charles Dickens was there in 1844, and wrote of his impressions in a little book he entitled *Pictures from Italy.* Let us leave the ancient world in its ruins and see from the other side of history, times much closer to our own, how that old place still arouses disgust and awe.

Excerpt from *Pictures from Italy*
By Charles Dickens

It is no fiction, but plain, sober, honest Truth, to say: so suggestive and distinct is it [the Colosseum] at this hour: that, for a moment—actually in passing in— they who will, may have the whole great pile before them, as it used to be, with thousands of eager faces staring down into the arena, and such a whirl of strife, and blood, and dust going on there, as no language can describe. Its solitude, its awful beauty, and its utter desolation, strike upon the stranger the next moment, like a softened sorrow; and never in his life, perhaps, will he be so moved and overcome by any sight, not immediately connected with his own affections and afflictions.

To see it crumbling there, an inch a year; its walls and arches overgrown with green; its corridors open to the day; the long grass growing in its porches; young trees of yesterday, springing up on its ragged parapets, and bearing fruit: chance produce of the seeds dropped there by the birds who build their nests within its chinks and crannies; to see its Pit of Fight filled up with earth, and the peaceful Cross planted in the centre; to climb into its upper halls, and look down on ruin, ruin, ruin, all about it; the triumphal arches of Constantine, Septimus Severus, and Titus; the Roman Forum; the Palace of the Caesars; the temples of the old religion, fallen down and gone; is to see the ghost of old Rome, wicked, wonderful old city, haunting the very ground on which its people trod. It is the most impressive, the most stately, the most solemn, grand, majestic, mournful sight, conceivable. Never, in its bloodiest prime, can the sight of the gigantic Coliseum, full and running over with the lustiest life, have moved one's heart, as it must move all who look upon it now, a ruin. GOD be thanked: a ruin![159]

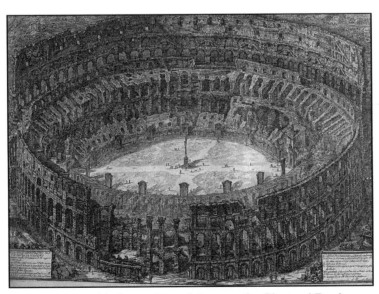

Colosseum with the stations of the cross by Giovanni Battista Piransei, c. 1750.

ENDNOTES

[1] Dorothy L. Sayers. "The Greatest Drama Ever Staged." In "Apologetics: Does God Exist." *Christian Broadcasting Network*. 2010. Web. 13 May 2016.

[2] Yoni Oppenheim. "The Origins of Jewish Performance from Prohibition to Precedent." *My Jewish Learning*. n.d. Web. 13 May 2016.

[3] M. Seligsohn. "Drama, Hebrew." *The Jewish Encyclopedia*. Ed. Isidore Singer. New York: Funk, 1903. 4.648. Print.

[4] Seligsohn. 4:648.

[5] Plato. *The Republic*. 3.401. In *The Dialogues of Plato*. Trans. Benjamin Jowett. London: Macmillan, 1802. 3.88. Print.

[6] Marcus Tullius Cicero. *On the Orator*. 1.4. In *Cicero on Oratory and Orators with His Letters To Quintus and Brutus*." Trans. J. S. Watson. London: Bohn, 1855. 147. Print.

[7] Cicero. 1.61.

[8] Aristotle. *Poetics*. 1.4. Trans. Trans. S. H. Butcher. London: Macmillan, 1895. Kindle file.

[9] College of Visual and Performing Arts. "Statement of Artistic Expression." University of Mary Hardin-Baylor. 4 Oct. 2005. Web. 13 May 2016.

[10] "Ledger Went Bat Crazy Preparing for Joker Role." *Yahoo Ireland &UK.*. 28 Nov. 2007. Web. 6 Aug. 2008.

[11] Olly Richards. "World Exclusive: The Joker Speaks." *Empire Online*. 28 Nov. 2007. Web. 11 May 2016.

[12] *The English Cyclopaedia: A Dictionary of Universal Knowledge*. Ed. Charles Knight. London, 1861. 8.191. Print.

[13] *Vitruvius: The Ten Books on Architecture*. Trans. Morris Hickey Morgan. Cambridge: Harvard UP, 1914. 1.9. Print.

[14] Philip Ball. "Why the Greeks Could Hear Plays from the Back Row." Lab for Ultrasonic NDE. Georgia Institute of Technology. 23 Mar. 2007. Web. 22 Mar. 2016.

[15] Plato. *The Republic*. 2.377. Trans. Benjamin Jowett. Oxford: Clarendon, 1888. 59. Print.

[16] Plato. 2.378.

[17] Plato. 10.604.

[18] Aristotle. 3.26.

[19] Aristotle. 2.15.

[20] Aristotle. 2.15.

[21] Aristotle. 1.4

[22] Aristotle. 2.13.

[23] Aristotle. 2.14.

[24] Aeschylus. *The Persians*. Trans. Robert Potter. London, 1893. Kindle file.

[25] Charles Gray. "Epistle to ALJ." *Poems*. Cupar, Fife: Tullis, 1811. 86.

[26] Dave Wilton. "Old English in LoTR." *Word Origins*. 1 Dec. 2002. Web. 14 Mar. 2016.

[27] Aeschylus. *Agamemnon*. Trans. E. D. A. Morshead. Harvard Classics. New York: Collier, 1901. 8.1.660-78. Print.

[28] Aristotle. 2.18.

[29] "*The Suda's* Life of Sophocles (Sigma 815): Text, Translation, and Commentary with Sources." Trans. William Blake Tyrell. *Electronic Antiquity*. 9.1, 103. 2006. Web. 15 Mar. 2016.

[30] William Willis Moseley. *The Quantity and Music of the Greek Chorus Discovered*. Oxford, 1847. 35. Print.

[31] Hugh Blair. *Lectures on Rhetoric and Belles Lettres*, London, 1818. 3.95. Print.

[32] Richard Green Moulton, ed. *Select Masterpieces of Biblical Literature: The Modern Reader's Bible: A Series of Works from the Sacred Scriptures Presented in Modern Literary Form*. London: Macmillan, 1898. 155-56. Print.

[33] Aristotle. 1.6.

[34] Aeschylus. *Prometheus Bound*. In *Four Plays by Aeschylus*. Trans. G. M. Cookson. Oxford: Blackwell, 1922. 175. Print.

[35] Aristotle 2.15.

[36] Aristotle. 2.14.

[37] Aristotle. 2.14.

[38] "Epicharmus of Syracuse Fragments." Trans. Kathleen Freeman. Cambridge: Harvard UP, 1948. *Demonax: Hellenic Library Beta*. 2013. Web. 18 Mar. 20016.

[39] Aristophanes. *The Birds*. Trans. Benjamin Bickley Rogers. London: Bell, 1919. Kindle file.

[40] Aristotle. 1.4.

[41] F. Storr translation.

[42] Susan B. Matheson. "The Mission of Triptolemus and the Politics of Athens." *Greek, Roman, and Byzantine Studies*. Vol. 35.4. (1994): 348. Duke University Libraries. CC By 3.0. n.d. Web. 2 Mar. 2016.

[43] William Congreve. *The Mourning Bride*. London: n. pub., 1697. *WikiSource*. 2 Feb. 2013. Web. 2 Mar. 2016.

[44] Robin Mitchell-Boyask. *Plague and the Athenian Imagination: Drama, History, and the Cult of Asclepius*. Cambridge: Cambridge UP, 2008. 111-12. Print.

[45] Sophocles. *Antigone*. In *Sophocles: The Plays and Fragments*. Trans. Richard Jebb. Cambridge: Cambridge UP, 1906. 95. Print.

[46] Lowell Edmunds. *Theatrical Space and Historical Place in Sophocles'* Oedipus at Colonus. Lanham: Rowman, 1996. 165-66. Print.

[47] William Blake Tyrrell. "Biography." *Brill's Companion to Sophocles*. Ed. Andreas Markantonatos. Leiden: Brill, 2012. 36. Print.

[48] Sophocles. *Philoctetes*. 251-316. Trans. George Theodoridis. *Bacchicstage*. 2009. Web. 12 May 2016. Used with permission.

[49] T. W. C. Edwards. Εὐριπίδου Ἑκάβη. *The Hecuba of Euripides*. London: Iley, 1822. 12-13. Print.

[50] Aristophanes. Lysistrata. 47-49. Trans. Jack Lindsay. London: Franfrolico, 1926. *Perseus Digital Library*. Tufts University. n.d. Web. 16 May 2016.

[51] Aristophanes. *The Clouds*. In *The Eleven Comedies*. Trans. Anonymous. London: Athenian, 1912. 1.7-8. Sam Houston State University. n.d. Web. 16 May 2016.

[52] Plato. *The Apology of Socrates*. In *The Apology, Phaedo, and Crito*. Trans. Benjamin Jowett. Harvard Classics. New York: Collier, 1910. Print.

[53] Plutarch. *Moralia*. 854.4. *Delphi Complete Works of Plutarch*. Delphiclassics.com. 2013. Web. 16 May 2016.

[54] Menander. *Dyskolos (Grouch)*. 795-805. Trans. Vincent J. Rosivach. *Fairfield.edu*. n.d. Web. 17 May 2016.

[55] Quintilian. Institutes of Oratory. Trans. H. E. Butler. Loeb Classical Library. Boston: Harvard UP, 1920-22. Penelope. University of Chicago. 4.10.1. 19 Nov. 2012. Web. 12 May 2016.

[56] Plutarch. Moralia. 853.3 The Complete Works of Plutarch. Delphi Classics. 2003. Web. 12 May 2016.

[57] Trans. E. D. A. Morshead. London: Kegan Paul, 1881. Kindle file.

[58] Charles W. Elliott, ed. Nine Greek Dramas by Aeschylus, Sophocles, Euripides, Aristophanes. Harvard Classics. New York: Collier, 1909. 8.440. Print.

[59] Elliott, 8.454.

[60] Aeschylus. *The Persians*. 659-60. Trans. Herbert Weir Smyth. Cambridge, MA: Harvard UP, 1926. *Perseus Digital Library*. Tufts University. n.d. 17 May 2016.

[61] Aeschylus. *The Suppliant Maidens*. 234-41. Trans. Herbert Weir Smyth.

[62] For a discussion of performances in the orchestra as opposed to the "stage," see John Pickard, "The Relative Position of Actors and Chorus in the Greek Theatre of the V Century B. C. Part I. Consideration of the Extant Theatres." *The American Journal of Philology*. 1893. 14.68-69.

[63] *Heraclidae*. Trans. Theodore Alois Buckley. *The Tragedies of Euripides*. New York: Harper, 1877. 285-86. Print.

[64] *Heraclidae*. 290-91.

[65] Euripides. *Helen*. Trans. Edward P. Coleridge. *The Plays: An English Translation. English Prose, from the Text of Paley*. 1912. Reprint. London: Forgotten Books, 2013. 1.350. Print.

[66] Euripides. *Iphegenia at Aulis*. Trans. Edward P. Coleridge. 2.408-409.

[67] Trans. H. W. Smyth. London: Heineman, 1926. 2.75. Print.

[68] Trans. H. W. Smith. 2.11, 13.

[69] Aristotle. 1.6.

[70] Pollux, Julius. *Extracts Concerning the Greek Theatre and Masks, Translated from the Greek of Julius Pollux*. London, 1775. *Eighteenth Century Collections Online*. Gale. Saint Louis University. n.d. Web. 11 Feb. 2016.

[71] Euripides. *Medea*. Trans. E. P. Coleridge. 1.38-40.

[72] Sophocles. *Antigone*. In *Sophocles: Oedipus the King, Oedipus at Colonnus, Antigone*. Trans. Francis Storr. London: Heinemann, 1912. 1. 319, 321. Print.

[73] Timothy Watchem. *War-horseiana: Or, An Authentic Report of the Sayings and Doings of the War Horse and His Ponies*. n.p. 1851. 17.

[74] New York: Bantam, 2005. 333-38.

[75] Hermogenes. "Preliminary Exercises Attributed to Hermogenes." 18. In *Progymnasmata: Greek Textbooks of Prose Composition and Rhetoric*. Ed. George Alexander Kennedy. Brill: Leiden, 2003. 83. Print.

[76] Sophocles. *Oedipus at Colonus*. Trans. Francis Storr. 1.213, 215, 217.

[77] Euripides. *Hecuba*. Trans. E. P. Coleridge. London: Bell, 1891. *Internet Sacred Text Archive*. n. d. Web. 24 Feb. 2016.

[78] Aeschylus. *Prometheus Bound*. In *Four Plays of Aeschylus*. Trans. G. M. Cookson. Oxford: Blackwell, 1912. 212. Print.

[79] Aeschylus. *Prometheus Bound*. 1116-25. *The Plays of Aeschylus*. Trans. Walter Headlam. London: Bell, 1909. 38. Print.

[80] Aeschylus. *Prometheus Bound*. Trans. Henry David Thoreau. Dia Art Foundation. *Diaart.org*. n.d. Web. 17 May 2016.

222

[81] Plutarch. "The Life of Pericles." *Plutarch's Lives*. Trans. John White. Rev. A. H. Clough. Boston: Little, 1895. 329-30. Print.

[82] Plutarch, 330.

[83] Plutarch, 329.

[84] George, Lord Lyttleton. "Dialogue XXIII: Pericles – Cosmo de Medicis, the First of That Name." *Dialogues of the Dead*. London: Cassel, 1889. 134. Print.

[85] Plutarch, 337-38.

[86] Janine Bakker. "Persian Influence on Greece (3)." *Livius.org: Articles on Ancient History*. n.d. Web. 24 Mar. 2016.

[87] Bakker.

[88] Plutarch. "Demetrius." *Lives of the Noble Grecians and Romans*. Trans. John Dryden. Ed. A. H. Clough. Boston: Little, 1906. 5.131. Print.

[89] Plutarch. 5.107.

[90] Plutarch. 5.107.

[91] Plutarch. 5.107.

[92] Plutarch. "Pompey." 2.41.

[93] Tertullian. *De Spectaculis*. Trans. S. Thelwall. 1869. *Ante-Nicene Fathers*. Edinburgh, 1885. 3.10. Print.

[94] E. Littel, ed.. *Littel's Living Age*. Boston: Little, 1856. 49.288. Print.

[95] William Shakespeare. *Julius Caesar*. 190-93. In *The Complete Works of Shakespeare*. Chicago: Scott, 1961. 787. Print.

[96] George Gordon, Lord Byron. *Childe Harold's Pilgrimage: A Romaunt*. London: Murray, 1812. 395. Print.

[97] John Chetwode Eustace. *A Tour Through Italy, Exhibiting a View of Its Scenery, Its Antiquities, and Its Monuments, Particularly as They are Objects of Classical Interest and Elucidation with an Account of the Present State of Its Cities and Towns and Occasional Observations on the Recent Spoliations of the French*. London, 1813. 1.277-78. Print.

[98] Juvenal. Satire 10:77-81. *Juvenal and Persius*. Trans. G. G. Ramsay. London: Heinemann, 1928. 198-99. Print.

[99] Pliny the Elder. *Natural History*. 36.24. In *Natural History: A Selection*. Trans. John F. Healey. London: Penguin, 1991. 357. Print.

[100] Pliny. Trans. John F. Healey. 357-58.

[101] Pliny. *Pliny's Natural History*. 8.50. Trans. Philemon Holland. London, 1847. 50. Print.

[102] Cassius Dio. *Roman History*. 10.6. Trans. Earnest Cary and Herbert B. Foster. Loeb Classical Library. 7.410. Print.

[103] Martial. *The Epigrams of Martial*. 28. Ed. Henry G. Bohn. London: Bell, 1890. 19. Print.

[104] Cassius Dio. 43.23. 253.

[105] Martial. *On the Public Shows of Domitian*. 7.5-6. *Tertullian.org*. n.d. Web. 17 May 2016.

[106] Martial. *On the Public Shows*. 221.

[107] Strabo. *Geography*. 6.2.6. In *Greek Texts and Translations*. *Perseus*. University of Chicago. n.d. Web. 17 May 2016.

[108] Tertullian. *The Apology of Tertullian*. 14. Trans. William Reeve. London, 1709. *Tertullian.org*. n.d. Web. 17 May 2016.

[109] Ovid. *Tristia ex Ponto*. 2.497. Trans. Arthur Leslie Wheeler. Cambridge: Harvard UP, 1939. 92. Print.

[110] Dorothea R. French. "Maintaining Boundaries: The Status of Actresses in Early Christian Society." *Vigiliae Christianae*. Aug. 1998. 296-97. Print.

[111] Tacitus. *The Annals*. 1.77. Trans. John Church and William Jackson Brodribb. London, 1869. 50. Print.

[112] Tacitus. 4.14. 152.

[113] Ovid. *Tristia ex Ponto*. 2.495, 515. 92, 94.

[114] Pliny the Younger. *Letters of Gaius Plinius Caecilius Secundus*. Trans. William Melmoth. Rev. F. C. T. Bosanquet. *The Harvard Classics*. (New York: Collier, 1909). 9.364-65. Print.

[115] French, 304, citing C.Th. 15.7.4 and 15.7.2.

[116] *Theodosian Code*. 15.7.4. In *Roman Civilization: Selected Readings*. Ed. Naphtali Lewis and Meyer Reinhold. New York: Columbia UP, 1990. 2.608. Print.

[117] Charalambos Bakirtzies, "Late Antiquity and Christianity in Thessalonikē: Aspects of a Transformation." *From Roman to Early Christian Thessalonike: Studies in Religion and Archaeology*. Eds. Laura Nasrallah, Charalambos Bakirtzis, and Steven J. Friesen. *Harvard Theological Studies 64*. Cambridge: Harvard UP, 2010. 413.

[118] "Martyr Adalion the Actor." *Orthodox Church in America*. 14 Apr. 2001. Web. 29 Apr. 2016.

[119] Michael D. Jordan. "St. Porphyrios the Mimic." *St. Seraphim of Sarov Eastern Orthodox Cathedral*. n.d. Web. 29 Apr. 2016.

[120] John of Chrysostom. *The Homilies of John of Chrysostom, Archbishop of Constantinople, on the Gospel of St. Matthew*. Oxford: Parker, 1894. 2. 542-47. Print.

[121] St. Augustine. *Confessions*. 3.2. Trans. R. S. Pine-Coffin. London: Penguin, 1961. 56. Print.

122 St. Augustine. *City of God*. 2.8. Trans. Marcus Dods. In *A Select Library of the Nicene and Post-Nicene Fathers of the Christian Church*. Ed. Philip Schaf. Buffalo: Christian Literature, 1887. 27. Print.

123 H. Goll. "Rome's Greatest Actor." *The Galaxy*. 16.1. (Jul 1873): 122. Print.

124 Cicero. *De Natura Deorum (On the Nature of the Gods)*. 1.28.

125 Cicero. *De Natura Deorum (On the Nature of the Gods)*. 1.28.

126 Cicero. *Cicero on Oratory and Orators with Letters*. 288.

127 H. Goll. 125.

128 Cicero. *De Oratore (On Oratory)*. 1.28

129 Theodosian Code. 15.7.4. In *Roman Civilization: Selected Readings*. Ed. Naphtali Lewis and Meyer Reinhold. 3rd ed. New York: Columbia UP, 1990. 608. Print.

130 Cicero. *De Oratore (On Oratory)*. 3.26.

131 Seneca. *Moral Letters to Lucilius*. 54.1. Trans. Richard Mott Gummere. London: Heinemann, 1918-25. 1. Print.

132 Roman History. 59.19.

133 Seneca. "On Clemency." 14. In *Minor Dialogs Together with the Dialog "On Clemency."* Trans. Aubrey Stewart. Bohn's Classical Library Edition. London: Bell, 1900. *Wikisource*. 21 Mar. 2015. Web. 18 May. 2016.

134 Seneca. "To Novatus on Anger." 1.2. In *Seneca: Moral Essays*. Trans. John W. Basore. London: Heinemann, 1928. 1.111. Print.

135 Tacitus. *Annals*. 15.64. Trans. John Church and William Jackson Brodribb. London: Macmillan, 1906. 314. Print.

136 *Boccaccio's Expositions on Dante's* Comedy, *Canto IV*. Trans. Michael Papio. Toronto: U of Toronto P, 2009. 235. Print.

137 Andrew F. West. "On a Patriotic Passage in the *Miles Gloriosus* of Plautus." *American Journal of Philology*. 8 (1887):15-33. *JSTOR*. Web. 19 Apr. 2016.

138 Plautus. *Miles Gloriosus*. 2.2. *The Comedies of Plautus*. Trans. Henry Thomas Riley. (London: Bohn, 1852). 79. Print.

139 Plautus. *The Casket Comedy*. 4.2. Trans. Paul Nixon. London: Heinemann, 1917. 5.171, 173.

140 Mary R. Lefkowitz and Maureen B. Fant. "Exposure of a Female Child. Oxyrhynchus, Egypt, 1 B.C." Oxyrhynchus papyrus 744. G. *Women's Life in Greece and Rome*. *The Stoa Consortium*. n. d. Web. 12 May 2016.

141 Seneca the Younger. *Of Anger*. 1.15. *Wikisource*. 16 May 2013. Web. 12 May 2016.

142 *The Didache: The Lord's Teaching to the Heathen by the Twelve Apostles*. 2.2. *StGemma.com Web Productions*. 2005-2011. Web. 12 May 2016.

143 Benjamin Wiker. "The Collapse of Europe: Child Abandonment and the Hope of the Church." *National Catholic Register*. 14 Aug. 2012. Web. 12 May 2016.

144 Dictionary of Greek and Roman Biography and Mythology. Ed. William Smith. Boston: Little, 1870. 3:997.

145 Luther, Martin. Selections from Table Talk. 1886. Reprint. London: Forgotten Books, 2013. 96. Print.

146 Terence. *The Eunuch*. 2.3. *The Comedies of Terence and the Fables of Phaedrus*. Trans. Henry Thomas Riley. 2.3. (London: Bohn, 1853). 33. Print.

147 Terence. *Adelphi: The Brothers*. 1.1. Trans. Henry Thomas Riley. *Perseus*. Tufts. n.d. Web. 20 May 2016.

148 All quotations in this exercise are from Seneca the Younger. *Thyestes*. *Seneca's Tragedies*. Trans. Frank Justus Miller. London: Heinemann, 1917. 2.139-40. Print.

149 Flavius Josephus. *Antiquities of the Jews*. 15.8.1 In *The Works of Flavius Josephus*. Trans. William Whiston, Cincinnati: Applegate, 1850. 315. Print.

150 Flavius Josephus. 15.8.4. 316.

151 Monika Kupper and Huw Jones. "Gladiators' Graveyard Discovered." *BBC News*. 2 May 2007. Web. 20 May 2016.

152 "Theater of Ephesus." *Sacred Destinations*. n.d. Web. 19 May 2016.

153 W. M. Ramsay. *The Church in the Roman Empire*. New York: Putnam, 1893. 152. Print.

154 Stephen Vincent Benét. *John Brown's Body*. Garden City, NY: Doubleday, 1928. 58. Print.

155 Suetonius. "The Life of Nero." *The Lives of the Twelve Caesars*. Trans. J. C. Rolfe. The Loeb Classical Library. (London: Heinemann, 1914). 2.20. Print.

156 Suetonius. 2.23.

157 Suetonius. 2.23-24.

158 Suetonius. 2.24.

159 Charles Dickens. *Pictures from Italy*. London, 1846. 167. Print.

Image Attribution

Images in the public domain requiring no attribution are not listed.

<u>Chapter 1</u>
Dance of Miriam. Public domain. PD-US.
The prophet David rebukes Miriam. Public domain. PD-US.
Quintilian. Public domain. PD-US.
Plato's Academy. Public domain. PD-US.
Cicero. Public domain. PD-US.
Russian icon of Mark the Evangelist. Public domain. PD-US.
Murder of Archbishop Thomas Becket. Public domain. PD-US.
Othello and Desdemona. Public domain. PD-US.

<u>Chapter 2</u>
Student performance of *Beauty and the Beast*. By soaringbird. *Flikr*. CC BY-SA 2.0. 20 Mar. 2010. Web. 13 May 2016.
The Orchestra Pit. By Everett Shin. Public domain. PD-US.
Thrust Stage at the Pasant, Michigan State University. Wikimedia. CC BY-SA 3.0. 18 Feb. 2014. Web. 24 May 2016.
Irving Berlin, Richard Rodgers, Oscar Hammerstein II, and Helen Tamiris watching auditions at the St. James Theatre. Library of Congress Digital ID: cph 3c26707.
Curtain call at Don Giovanni Opera, Australia 2014. *Wikimedia Commons*. CC BY-SA 4.0. 6 Sept. 2014. Web. 13 May 2016.
The French mime Jyjou*. *Wikimedia Commons*. CC BY-SA 2.0. 3 June 2013. Web. 24 May 2016.
Lady Macbeth's soliloquy performed by Ellen Terry. Public domain. PD-US.
Robert Cohen. CC BY SA-3.0. *Wikimedia Commons*. CC BY-SA 3.0. 1 Mar. 2008. Web. 24 May 2016.
Eliza Doolittle as portrayed by Ingeborg von Kusserow. *Wikimedia Commons*. CC BY-3.0 DE. 16 Apr. 2009. Web. 13 May 2016.
Battle of Culloden. By David Morier. PD-US.

<u>Chapter 3</u>
Sketch of Theatre of Dionysus at Athens. J. H. Breasted. *History of Europe: Ancient and Medieval*. Boston: Ginn, 1914. 147. Print.
Photo of Theatre of Dionysus at Athens. Templar 52. *el.wikipedia*. 10 Oct. 2007. Web. 27 May 2016.
Ancient Greek Theatre. *Wikimedia Commons*. CC BY 3.0. 12 Dec. 2009. Web. 21 Mar. 2016.

<u>Chapter 4</u>
Ajax. By J. C. Andrä. Public Domain. PD-US.
Oedipus and the Sphinx. Tondo of an Attic red-figure kylix, 480-470 BC. From Vulci. Museo Gregoriano Etrusco, room XIX. Photog. Juan José Moral. Public Domain. *Wikimedia Commons*. 27 Feb. 2009. Web. 17 Mar. 2016.
Greek Chorus in a performance of *Edipo Rei*. Ies Manuel Garcia Barros a Estrada-Pontevedra. *Wikimedia Commons*. CC By 2.0. 13 June 2012. Web. 15 Mar. 2016.
Pottery image of a Chorus of stilt-walkers. James Logie Memorial Collection, University of Canterbury, New Zealand. Photog. Remi Mathis. *Wikimedia Commons*. CC BY-SA 3.0. 24 Nov. 2011. Web. 15 Mar. 2016.
Greco-Roman trispastos. *Wikimedia Commons*. CC BY-SA 4.0. 17 Nov. 2010. Web. 24 May 2016.
Roman Theatre at Bosra, Syria. *Wikimedia Commons*. CC BY-SA 3.0. 13 Nov. 2005. Web. 24 May 2016.
Satan baptizing his followers. *Wikimedia Commons*. PD-1996.

<u>Chapter 5</u>
Aeschylus. Public domain. PD-US.
Sophocles. *Wikimedia Commons*. CC BY-SA 3.0. 26 Dec. 2008. Web. 24 May 2016.
Young Sophocles Leading the Chorus. Public domain. PD-US.
Rod of Aesclepius. *Wikimedia Commons*. CC BY-SA 3.0. 14 Aug. 2009. Web. 24 May 2016.
Marble Slab with the Recall of Philoctetes. Archaeological Museum of Braurum. PD-US.
Pankration. *Simple Wikipedia*. CC By 2.5. 4 Mar. 2011. Web. 1 Mar. 2016.
Molossian hound (British Museum). *Wikimedia Commons*. CC By 2.5. 24 Jun 2011. Web. 1 Mar. 2016.
Aristophanes. Public domain. PD-US.
Socrates in a Basket. Public domain. PD-US.
Plutarch's *Moralia*. Public domain. PD-US.

<u>Chapter 6</u>
Chiton and Himation. Public domain. PD-US.
Peplos. *Wikimedia Commons*. CC BY-SA 3.0. 7 Feb. 2011. Web. 24 May 2016.
Xanthias and Heracles on Greek vase. *Wikimedia Commons*. CC BY-SA 2.5. 19 Aug. 2007. Web. 24 May 2016.
Statue of Darius I. Fabien Dany. www.fabiendany.com. *Wikimedia Commons*. CC BY-2.5. 22 June 2006. Web. 17 May 2016.
Winged Victory with incense holder. By Sharon Mellerus. *Wikimedia Commons*. CC BY-2.0. 14 Oct. 2009. 24 May 2016.
Greek chariot depicted on Amathus sarcophagus. *Wikimedia Commons*. CC BY-2.0. 29 June 2009. Web. 24 May 2016.
Menander with theatre masks. Public domain. PD-US.
Sousse mosaic of a theatre mask. © Ad Meskens / *Wikimedia Commons*. CC BY-3.0. 21 Dec. 2012. Web. 13 May 2016.
New Comedy first slave mask. *Wikimedia Commons*. CCO 1.0 Universal PD. 30 Aug. 2015. Web. 24 May 2016.

Women's comic mask. Theatre mask dating from the 4th/3rd century BC. Giovanni Dall'Orto. *Wikimedia Commons*. 23 Jan. 2010. Web. 24 May 2016.

Chapter 7

Roman School. Relief found in Neumagen near Trier, a teacher with three discipuli. Around AD 180-185. Photo of casting in Pushkin museum, Moscow. Shakko/*Wikipedia*. CC BY-SA 3.0. 28 Apr. 2013. Web. 12 Feb. 2016.

Klara Zeigler as Medea. Public domain. PD-US.

Theatre mask. Antalya Archaeological Museum. Ancient Roman sarcophagus 2nd century BC. Wolgang Sauber. *Wikimedia Commons*. CC BY-3.0. 15 Dec. 2011. Web. 24 May 2016.

Theatre masks (clip art). Drama and the Night Owl Theatre Company. Kelowna Secondary School of Fine Arts. *Wikispaces*. 2016. Web. 12 Feb. 2016.

Electra. Female theatre mask from Pompeii. Public domain. PD-US.

Chapter 8

Pericles of Athens. Public domain. PD-US.

Hall of a Hundred Columns at Persepolis. Photog. Philippe Chavin. *Wikimedia Commons*. CC BY-SA 3.0. 16 Nov. 2006. Web. 24 Mar. 2016.

Chapter 9

Theatre at Aphrodisias, Turkey. Photog. Carole Addato. *Wikimedia Commons*. CC BY 2.0. 4 Apr. 2015. Web. 22 Mar. 2016.

Theatre of Pompey in Rome. 3-D Model by Lasha Tskhondia. *Wikimedia Commons*. CC BY 3.0. 1 Oct. 2012. Web. 24 Mar. 2016.

Musicians from Zliten mosaic. Public domain. PD-US.

Theatre at Epidaurus. *Wikimedia Commons*. CC BY 3.0. 14 July 2008. Web. 24 May 2016.

Roman Colosseum. Dennis Jarvis. *Flikr*. CC BY 2.0. 10 Oct. 2010. Web. 24 May 2016.

Mosaic depicting *bestiarii*. Public domain. PD-US.

Naumachia. Giovanni Lanfranco. Public domain. PD-US.

Augustine and Monica. Ary Scheffer. 1846. Public domain. PD-US.

Chapter 10

Juno Sospita. Public domain. PD-US.

Seneca the Younger. Calidius. *Wikimedia Commons*. CC BY 3.0. 24 July 2007. Web. 24 May 2016.

Mosaic of Roman theatre mask. Public domain. PD-US.

Paul before Gallico. FreeBibleImages.org. *Wikimedia Commons*. CC BY 3.0. n.d. Web. 24 May 2016.

Titus Maccius Plautus. Public domain. PD-US.

Terence. Public domain. PD-US.

Chapter 11

Annotated page of Terence's *Adelphoe* (act one, scene two). PD-US.

Theatre mask at Ostia Antica. Patrick Deneker. *Wikimedia Commons*. CC BY-2.0. 7 Apr. 2007. Web. 24 May 2016.

Chapter 12

Coin of Herod the Great. *Wikimedia Commons*. CC BY-SA 3.0. 25 July 2008. Web. 24 May 2016.

Bust of Flavius Josephus. Public domain. PD-US.

Theatre at Beit Shean. *Wikimedia Commons*. CC BY-SA 2.0. 17 Sept. 2014. Web. 19 May 2016.

Theatre at Ephesus. Thomas Brosnahan. *Turkey Travel Planner*. n.d. Web. 24 May 2016. Used with permission.

Map of Ephesus. *FreeBibleImages.com*. CC BY-SA 3.0. n.d. Web. 19 May 2016.

Cavea del teatro romano di Neapolis, ditto anche dell'Anticaglia (Theatre at Naples). City Class. *Wikimedia Commons*. CC BY-3.0. 23 Apr. 2012. Web. 24 Mar. 2016.

Quo Vadis: Nero and the Burning of Rome. Altemus Edition, 1897. Illustration by M. de Lipman. Public domain.

Colosseum with stations of the cross. Public domain. PD-US.

Licensing Links

CC BY-SA 1.0 https://creativecommons.org/licenses/by-sa/1.0/
CC BY-SA 2.0 https://creativecommons.org/licenses/by-sa/2.0/
CC BY-SA 3.0 https://creativecommons.org/licenses/by-sa/3.0/
CC BY-SA 4.0 https://creativecommons.org/licenses/by-sa/4.0/

Made in the USA
Lexington, KY
21 April 2017